# 10 STEPS
# TO A SUCCESSFUL
# BUSINESS

# 10 STEPS TO A SUCCESSFUL BUSINESS

### How Culture, Planning, Staffing, and Communication Can Make or Break a Company

## DANA McBRIEN

There are three individuals I'd like to dedicate this book to. All were influential in shaping my life, providing me the courage to be more than I would have ever thought myself capable of becoming, and/or inspiring me to place my thoughts on paper.

My first dedication is to my father. Though he has not been with us on Earth for quite some time, his influence will never fade. My dad, despite having numerous physical issues, never let those issues stand in the way of learning new trades, working hard, and raising a family. I can't ever remember a time when he complained that God had dealt him a bad hand; he looked at life as a true blessing. With his wife by his side as his ears (he was legally deaf), he lived a life more fulfilling than many. My dad taught a truly inspirational lesson to us of perseverance through his actions. It has also made me see the struggles others may be going through and appreciate how they are persevering.

My second dedication is to my mother (that might have been predictable). The lesson in life my mom taught through her actions was patience and dedication. While the lesson of patience may have skipped a generation with me, it still didn't go unnoticed. The love and true appreciation my mom and dad shared with each other were incredible. They lived their lives always there for each other. Even though mom is still with us and we have the opportunity to share how much she means to us, she will never truly know the inspiration she provides to her children, grandchildren, great-grandchildren, and great-great-grandchildren.

My last dedication is to my sister-in-law Susan. Her inspiration to put the many stories she intently listened to on paper is the reason this book was created. The stories I sometimes felt were somewhat mundane and normal she thought were interesting and unique. She provided the encouragement, prodding, and early editing that helped me across the finish line.

# Contents

# Acknowledgments

First, I'd like to thank my wife, who has always encouraged this dreamer to see his dreams through no matter how crazy they may have seemed at the time. She encouraged this unsure person to be the confident man sometimes only she could recognize. Her belief in me has been the most positive reinforcement in my life.

Second, I'd like to thank my family for their continued encouragement and support. My father and mother, who always worked hard and provided the best possible examples to enable me to be the best I can. My brother, Dennis, who believed I could be something even better and allowed me to participate with his older friends to make me tougher. And a special dedication to my sister, Diana (1947-2020), who was always such a strong believer in her "little brother." Her words of encouragement and constant compliments were always a boost to the ego . . . although I knew she was very biased. Diana always asked how my book was coming along. My procrastination in completing this writing meant additional world events and experiences could be added to the content, but, unfortunately, it also meant she would never get to read it.

Third, I'd like to thank past bosses and co-workers who both encouraged and supported my visions as they turned into realities. Their support and belief in me and my abilities spurred me to work even harder to ensure that success was achieved.

Last, but not least, I'd like to acknowledge all those leaders and workers who continue to believe in their company, through good times and bad times, and who work hard to make it the best it can be. It is your efforts, through sometimes-blind dedication, that inspire me to share my experiences. Keep it up ... You can do amazing things!

☊

# Prologue

As a final word of advice before getting started, I'd like to offer some additional insight into the types of organizations that thrive and survive. The strongest organizations I have worked in, observed, or led, have been those where open and blatantly honest communication existed. Egos were not permitted (understood rule). Everyone was seen for their value and contributions (equally). Employees would "take a bullet for" (not literally) the leaders of the organization because it was understood that the leaders would do the same for them. It is an organization which moves, thinks, and feels in unison *despite* any adversity which may exist.

Does this sound like Nirvana? It is! A leader's role transitions to working on innovating the business direction and focusing on happy customers instead of fixing and apologizing. An employee's focus is on doing great things for the good of the whole, instead of fearing failure and just putting in their time. They develop an understanding that the organization doesn't exist for them to benefit. They exist for the organization to benefit, and, in turn, they benefit as a result. My suggestion—try it! Each party has to contribute to make it happen. Dare to keep it simple in order to overcome the complexity your company faces!

Best of luck to you all!

"A Simple Man"

# Introduction

Whether you need to "Reboot," "Renovate," or "Reinvent" your business, following these Ten Steps can help redefine and refine your business. Along the journey, the reader can expect some self-assessment, introspection, soul-searching, and evaluation on both a personal and professional level. I want to warn that the journey may entail a lot of "Ah-hah!" moments, along with many "duh" outcomes. I hope the content of my writing can reach anyone from a small-business owner to a CEO, from a middle-management representative to a direct line leader, from an office worker to a construction worker, and everyone in between. I hope you also recognize some activities as something you could apply as a parent, and I may call some of those out. No matter your title, education, or "status" within a working business ecosystem, I hope you will recognize that *everyone* can contribute to success or failure—whether you believe it or not. I think you will find this to be true for any type of unit working together.

"Ah-hah!" moments may come from digging deep into the inner workings of your business. It may be as simple as someone *finally* explaining *why* you do something, and always have, without providing an explanation. Many "duh" responses may, in fact, lead you to "Ah-Hah!" moments when you least expect it. All it takes to discover these moments is an open mind and a little thick skin when the problem or condition turns out to be you or something you have championed, created, or invested in. As I'll allude to in different parts of our journey, there are no bad actions when trying to work out the best situation for any business—with the exception of the one preceded by "in." Inaction in any business can be the bane of the bottom line, the monkey that disrupts morale, and, ultimately, the enigma which ends your business.

With all of this in mind, let's begin the initial phase of the journey toward "better." Whether your "better" entails better profit, better customer satisfaction, better product, better processes, or better morale, this book will provide you with revelations that help in your understanding and ultimately give insight into how you can accomplish it.

Ω

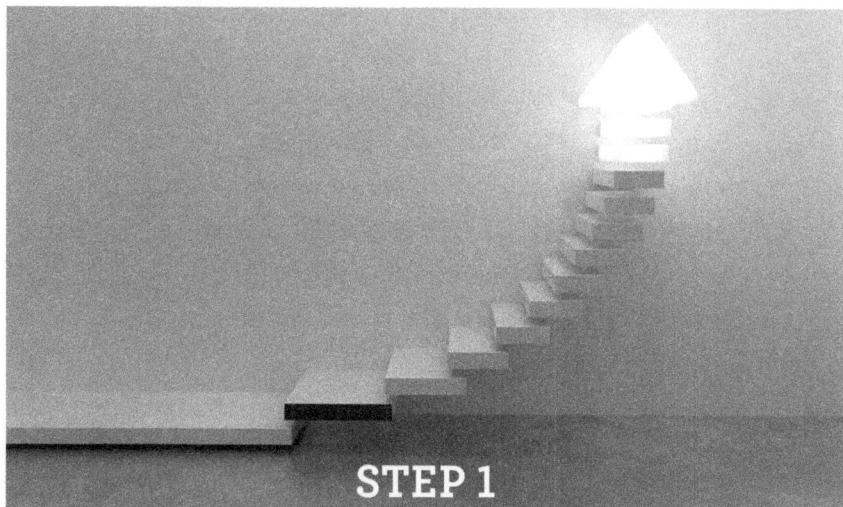

STEP 1

# Assessing Your Company's Health

*In this Step:*

- Assessing the company's financial and cultural health
- Learning from the past
- Understanding where your energy is spent
- Assessing the business strategy
- Analyzing the state of your business assets

## FINANCIAL HEALTH VS. CULTURAL HEALTH

Let's start with the health of your bottom line. If you are currently experiencing healthy profits, you may think about skipping this discussion.

*Don't!*

A healthy bottom line is not always an indication of the health of the organization. If your CFO or Accountant is singing the "Happy Song" because you've just experienced improved, growing, or record profits, you should still dare to ask *Why? What changed?* You might

1

want to take the newfound wealth of your company, your nice profit-sharing, or special bonus check and run as fast as you can. After all, you should never look a gift horse in the mouth, right? Wrong! *Conditional profits* (those spurred by external events or conditions you can't control when they influence in a negative way) may be masking deep-rooted problems or a looming disaster. For example:

Let's say your organization's return on sales improved from 8% to 10%. Great results. Go on—take the money and run! But a significant influence is felt from a positive foreign-exchange position which netted you a 4% bonus. Still happy? I hope not! You can apply that level of analysis to anything you manage . . . a manager's budget, a buyer's commodity oversight. You get the picture. Don't get lulled into a false sense of security because the bottom line improved. Make sure you understand why, so you don't receive an unpleasant surprise next month, next year, or the year after that. Many have experienced this recently. Riding the wave of a very good economic condition, with no true downturn in sight, suddenly, the spigot was turned off, and the wave was gone. Nothing like a disaster such as COVID-19 to gain an understanding of where you truly stand. This is your "financial health" statement.

The second half of this health check is the cultural health of the business. Imagine if you built your business structure in the sand. Building a foundation in sand requires some deep pilings, and most businesses are not going to invest that type of money just to establish themselves. A standard foundation built in sand will ultimately lead to the structure crumbling, sinking, or falling over. It's best to have a solid foundation and build it on solid ground. The foundation relates to your most valued asset . . . people. The best foundation that motivates and retains people does not involve the almighty dollar. The truly sustainable motivator for people is a sense of belonging and a sense of contribution to something great.

In my humble opinion, that sense can be established within a company only with a strong cultural-belief system. This creates a completely opposite outcome than building in the sand. Having a strong culture can be likened to building the business's foundation on stable and structurally sound ground. It is with the belief system that you conduct your business. It is the principles by which you interact with each other. It can motivate people to feel they belong to something great!

Similar to the assessment of the company's financial health, cultural health should be understood to ensure there aren't problems hiding in the weeds. I'll address more aspects of a business's culture during the next Step.

One way to assess the culture of an organization is to better understand what steers it toward its established goals and objectives. To say a company should not be concerned about profit would be like saying a human should not be concerned about oxygen. Without it, the entity ceases to exist. When an organization becomes consumed by profit is when its culture begins to suffer. If you or your organization is driven solely by profit, this is the first sign of becoming unhealthy. This is when decisions can be driven away from doing what is "right" and toward doing what is "right for the bottom line." If you find during the initial assessment of your environment that you seem to be doing more of what is right for the bottom line, it is time to reverse course before the iceberg sinks your ship.

During the recent COVID-19 pandemic, the stories about companies keeping their employees on the payroll were heartening. Only after understanding the condition would continue on for an extended period of time did many of those companies determine they would have to furlough many, most, or all of those valuable assets to keep their business intact. The assistance from the federal government to help retain them on the payroll helped those who were fortunate enough to gain access. The number of companies who fought to keep their employees paid means there are those who already recognize what their most important assets really are.

An organization built on trust, honesty, integrity, and open communication is one with a good culture. The second assessment of a company culture should be to understand what motivates people. If the motivation is the same as an unhealthy organization and is found to be money, it is not sustainable. If it is truly the feeling of self-worth and the opportunity to be an integral part of something great, as a leader, you would be well advised to hold on to those employees! A team with that culture can accomplish just about anything the leaders can dream of. With the proper focus, education, and support, the sky is the limit. If the company's and people's beliefs align, look out!

## LOOKING FORWARD THROUGH THE PAST

Now that you have some idea of what is driving your financial and cultural health—and if it is what you would hope—it is time to understand more about your business. The title of this section implies how important it is to know where the business has come from in order to define where it should go. That may sound counterintuitive to some, but, hopefully, my thought behind this will become clearer as I explain this section.

A company's characteristics, evident from past actions, along with the business drivers and conditions, are important for knowing how the organization may react in the future. For example: If the business is a bakery, your vision and direction is dramatically different from those of a technology company. Keep this thought in mind while I explain the different "levels of drive" a company can adopt. The defined driver may or may not be right for the conditions you operate in. Even more important is to conduct continuing assessments of those conditions to ensure your actions match the current state you are operating in. Here are what I'll call the "Driven By" definitions to assess your business with:

### Driven by Status Quo

The best description of this condition would be *"If it ain't broke, don't fix it."* Not many industries today would admit that they are in this state, but I would guess there are some companies that, through a self-assessment, will find they are. Their condition could even be different based on the area of the business being assessed. Product development might be very aggressive, with a highly inventive approach, while all other areas of the business may be lacking the required movement to keep up with the current conditions. Be careful not to fall into the trap of defining your conditions based on only one or two areas within your own company or department. Similarly, don't hesitate to move different areas of the business into a different defining category. The business's product might belong in this category, but the distribution and supply-chain segments of the business may require a different approach.

Take the previous example: A bakery company's culture could be driven by the Status Quo. Over the years, the product has evolved, but the product lineup has stayed fairly stable. We still go to the grocery store and buy bread (most of us). The industry has likely been impacted by the low-carb/no-carb diet crazes, but there is still a bread aisle. Most companies have diversified while developing new products, but they would still fit in this category. If a technology company assessed themselves in this level of motivation, we would likely be saying in the near future, if not already, "Who was that company that used to make . . . ?" Even a bakery company needs to continue their assessment of business drivers and conditions. They need to ensure that outside influences, such as government regulations, health declarations, pricing challenges, and market influences haven't impacted them and created a need to reassess and move to a different "driver."

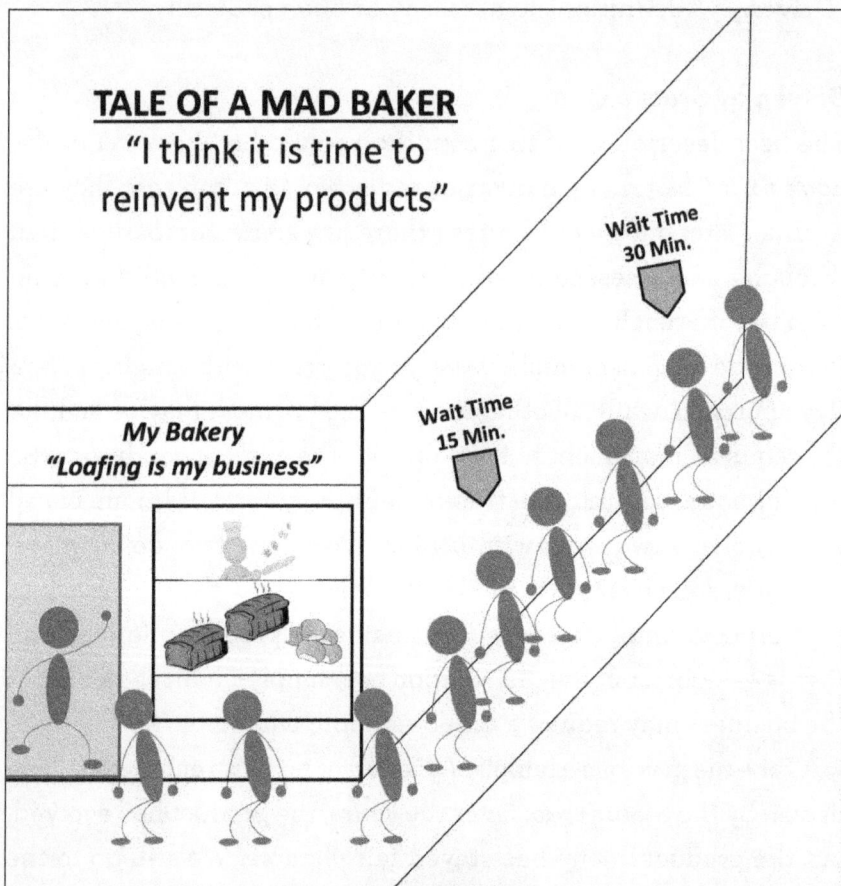

**TALE OF A MAD BAKER**
"I think it is time to reinvent my products"

Wait Time 30 Min.

Wait Time 15 Min.

*My Bakery*
*"Loafing is my business"*

Likewise, the amount of data analytics used by the different companies will vary greatly. For a stable product environment, the required data analytics can be relatively simple. Sales volumes by product type, by region, by season, and by demographics create the basis for their analytics. The number of transactions analyzed might be quite high, but the complexity of the analytics will likely remain fairly simple. For other types of industries, the analytics can become quite complicated. Within the product type, data on which features or options are most important can be invaluable for driving future development. Regional data may also define a market's climate or infrastructure needs.

Data analytics in a smaller business environment, as opposed to a larger one, are also very different. In a smaller organization, the complexity can be much lower but with a higher urgency or impact. Some metrics in that smaller environment can be captured through a visual confirmation. Productivity within an organization of 5 may not need to be captured in a metric like it is in an organization of 500, where employees don't sit within proximity of each other or the person assigned to supervise them. This is particularly relevant in the environment of remote working we find ourselves in now. Visibility is also important, as the result of potentially losing a customer could be quite impactful on the company's bottom line. The margin for error in a larger organization can make less of an impact but shouldn't be any less important. Adjusting the complexity of your data analytics to match the complexity of your business is important. I think you get the picture.

### Driven by Innovation

This is where both stability and chaos exist. In Status Quo motivation, segments of your business might be very stable, but other segments are being challenged by internal and/or external influences. When this situation exists, a company might need to innovate many segments of their existence to keep up with or overtake their competition. My experiences have shown that virtually every company belongs in this space in one way or another. Innovation might be necessary for a small portion of the business or in many different areas. A perfect example of an area where innovation should be applied in virtually every company is logistics. The influences from the trucking industry, labor conditions, and the effects of changing consumer expectations continuously place challenges on current supply-chain infrastructures. This is truer today than ever before. Whether you are a large company and design your logistics network or a smaller company that uses mostly parcel services, you have likely felt the impact in both cost and service levels.

If you find yourself in this area for the majority of your business, it could mean that you are unnecessarily messing with a good thing—or that, maybe, you really do belong there. Innovation is never a bad thing. In fact, it can become a core part of your business culture. An opportunity to bring about change in the organization is a great way to gain engagement from all your people and help them attain the ultimate feeling of belonging and that they are making a difference. Conversely, stifling these opportunities when the employees see them as necessary to sustain the business may create apathy or a feeling of disconnection in those same employees.

### Driven by Reinvention

A company driven by reinvention is one which is in an industry where products rapidly evolve. A company may be impacted by something for which there is no precedent. The COVID-19 pandemic will likely have organizations large and small, as well as many families, rethinking how they approach their daily lives. In this condition, stability is not part of their vocabulary. What sells today will be passé in a week. They are under attack from consumer habits. They are under attack from their competitors, who are launching better products immediately after you launch your own—new products you have just spent one to two years designing, testing, and marketing. They are under attack from conditions which are natural or unnatural, such as a pandemic.

Virtually all facets of their business (product development, finance, marketing, sourcing, supply chain) are in a state of chaos. Reinventing your business model is a way to apply some control to the chaos.

A company driven by reinvention may be an electronics company. They may not recognize it as a driver because it has become their way of life. This generally comes with a pretty large price tag, depending on the business involved. Imagine an auto company trying to live in the same environment as a cell-phone manufacturer. The cell-phone manufacturer has the next-generation phone in testing and development when they launch a new one. An auto company with a three- to five-year development cycle would find it difficult to keep up in that environment, not to mention unsustainably costly.

As in the Driven by Innovation environment, there will be times in a company's lifespan when some aspect of their business needs to go through reinvention. Identifying when is the right time to totally reinvent their sales and marketing (or another part of the business) is key. Having the right insight and continuous reassessment will help you succeed, and "letting it ride" will not. It is paramount for every organization to benchmark and network to understand what the competition is thinking as well as what new methods might be surfacing in other business verticals. Continuous education is necessary to make certain there are fresh ideas percolating in the organization.

> *"I am not talking about formal education through academia. I am talking about life experiences brought about by the belief there is more one doesn't know than they do know—you must have a true desire to learn."*

### Simply Driven

I'll start this area with a strong warning. If you are squeamish or easily frightened, you may want someone who isn't to read it for you and summarize. If you find your organization is working in this fashion, it could be very disturbing. The best way to define *Simply Driven* is a general feeling within the organization that *"We have to do something!"* The problem with this approach? It may not have a strong-enough path to achieve the desired result, if any exists at all. It may actually be necessary to stem the tide until a more permanent action can be defined. Additionally, the desired result may not even be known. You may just know that what is currently being done is not good enough—in a company, a department, an individual, or a government. A recent example of that was when the United States shut down travel of foreign visitors coming from infected areas of the world during the COVID-19 pandemic. At some point in our lives and/or careers, we all have been in this mode in one way or another.

This type of motivation can be extremely dangerous to an organization (there is a "Duh" moment). If it is so obvious, I wonder why it is so easy to fall into this trap? Why would a leader purposely jump down this rabbit hole knowing it is dangerous? It's simple: Sometimes, it is necessary when the only bad action is inaction. There are both leaders *and* employees who can pull this off very successfully. Sometimes it is absolutely necessary. If you approached a burning house and the only thing you have available to you is a bucket and a well, are you going to watch the house burn while you come up with a strategy? That is not human nature. You are going to start throwing buckets of water on the house while you adopt a different strategy as one becomes evident.

If you find your company or yourself in this mode frequently, it is probably time to rethink the strategy and slide into a more "innovative" or "reinventive" one. It may come with some short-term consequences. I'll go into a bit more detail in the next area as I discuss evaluating where you and your organization spend most of your energy.

### Where Does Your Energy Go?

All organizations have members who work harder than others. That is not what this conversation is about. Getting the total energy capacity up in the organization can be addressed through engagement and motivation, and will be talked about throughout this book. The next level of self-assessment I want to cover is centered around where your organization's current energy is spent.

The questions you have to ask yourselves are:

> Does my or my organization's energy get spent more on "fixing" things that aren't quite right or on "Innovating" things to move them forward?

> Does my or my organization's energy get spent more on "apologizing" for things that didn't turn out as planned or on "listening to praise" from my customers or peers for the things that did?

> Does my or my organization's energy get spent more on "catching up" to my competition or on "leading" my industry'?

If you answer the questions with the first definition versus the latter, there are several conditions that may be in play. Maybe you can't plan your way out of a wet paper bag. I doubt that. Maybe, as an organization *or* an individual, the focus is on looking at short-term gains over building sustainability and achieving long-term goals. Maybe you aren't focusing on the right things and are not understanding what stage of the business marathon your organization is in. Maybe the organization isn't listening to the voice of its customers closely enough. Are you innovating when you should? Are you reinventing your business or yourself when the time calls for it? If you find your organization with product sales slowing frequently, and you're offering incentives or deep discounts to move the inventory at a lower- or no-profit margin, the frequency of innovating may need to be increased.

In the last section, I probably made the *Simply Driven* option sound all bad, all the time. It can be bad but not always. If you are typically "fixing," "apologizing," or "catching up," you are likely making that energy use an integral part of your business plan. The *Simply Driven* option has a place in all businesses. Every business suffers some type of emergency condition. The *Simply Driven* approach can be deployed to get out of it. There are those who are good at using that tool effectively. There is a place and time to use this strategy. As mentioned in the COVID-19 example, doing nothing would have been worse.

The people utilized to create and deploy emergency actions may turn out to be the best long-term strategists a company can have. After all, if they are capable of coming up with a plan and implementing it, massaging it, and making it work without enough time to think about it, imagine what they could do given a little time to develop a company's strategy. Be careful: these people may, in fact, come up with ideas ahead of their time because their minds are typically running at a rate many can't keep up with. Discounting those strategies because they aren't immediately understood is a mistake. These strategies may become part of the company strategy years after they first were suggested, but at what lost opportunity cost or risk of being too late?

If you have assessed yourself in the Fix/Apologize/Catch Up condition, you have identified a problem that needs to be addressed. In order to get the organization out of that spiral, it will take everyone to redirect the energy. There must be buy-in from the investors or Board of Directors around the potential of temporarily reduced performance. There must be buy-in from the management team that performance measures temporarily will be missed. There must be buy-in from the employees that profit-sharing or raises may be temporarily reduced. They must all understand the long-term strategy the company is deploying to make things better soon!

## THE COMPANY'S ROAD MAP

The next level of assessment may become a little dicey, because it involves strategic planning for the organization. A company may believe their road map is extremely sound and characterizes the overall direction it needs to take. Now the dicey part: If that road map was created with a fixed end in mind and was established a year ago, two years ago, or three years ago and was written in ink, it may be obsolete by now. There are strategic endeavors in a company's business plan which can be considered timeless. They are the cornerstones of the company's foundation, and they are relevant regardless of where business conditions take it.

An example (hypothetical) of that type of planning would be to provide customers with products that promote person-to-person communication. They are the blueprints by which you establish that foundation. Conversely, there are many items in a company's business plan that *must* change with the conditions and require continuous monitoring to assess the need to adjust them—or, in the most extreme cases, eliminate them! An example (again hypothetical) of this would be to continue innovation of the telegraph equipment as a solution for person-to-person communication in the 21$^{st}$ century.

I hope you are sitting down, but believe it or not, sometimes there is no business plan. This can take place in any company, regardless of the size and scope. You might ask, "How in the world does that ever happen?" You might also be able to answer that question. The fact is, it can happen in a number of ways. It can happen because there isn't someone "assigned" or "in charge" of the business-planning process. When a company has to establish a business-planning

13

department, it may actually indicate an issue. It can imply there is a disconnect between the thoughts of the leaders and the teams that execute them. It can mean the leaders of the organization do not have a clear direction in mind for the organization. It can indicate a condition where leaders are not providing the right leadership required to make the strategic direction they wish to execute known to the organization. Not giving those individuals who are charged with executing a desired strategy what they need to accomplish it will result in inaction.

Assessment skills should help you understand where your organization stands. Here are several conditions which could be driving your company's direction:

### Direction Locked in the Leader's Head

This condition will most likely exist in a smaller- to medium-sized entity. This can be a good position for a company to be in. Removing distractions by not releasing too much detail will prompt the execution groups to keep their eye on the ball. It has long been said that the best way to eat an elephant (symbolic for a very large undertaking) is one bite at a time. Instead of focusing on "the elephant" before them, the teams can focus only on the portion they have been asked to consume. One danger with this approach is, if a leadership change occurs for any reason, the plan can be lost, without anyone understanding how the pieces they are responsible for fit into the full puzzle. Document it, periodically assess it, and adjust the plan and the components often.

As stated earlier, the intent of this book is to offer solutions that apply to a company scenario, a department within a company, or even to an individual's situation. An idea locked inside a leader's head can also be lost if they don't document it so that it stays in front of everyone. Understanding their defined goals and milestones helps them to know how they are truly doing.

The Psychic Boss

"I knew if I thought hard enough the business plan would be felt by everyone!"

### Boardroom Banter

This can be one of the more dangerous forms of business planning—when the bantering becomes just that. It can easily turn to ideas without action. It can also lead to action without understanding what the ideas are. Too many individuals with their own goals and agendas may stymie great ideas because they don't want to follow through on suggestions that weren't theirs. This type of organizational condition requires a strong leader to mediate the discussion and make the decisions required to ensure that an actionable plan exists.

This form of business-direction development *implies* that a documented strategy will be a byproduct, but it's not a guarantee. It also implies that, since there is a boardroom, the company is a larger organization, with a more complex ecosystem. Boardroom-produced output should be a directional-level strategy and should not limit the ways each part of the organization will execute to get there. In a larger organization, where a "Boardroom" exists, there may be an infrastructure capable of drawing the plans to execute the direction created there. That's not always the case. Presence of a "Boardroom" does not always mean that the organization is large, either.

"Great discussion everybody! We have no consensus business plan direction yet. We'll table the discussion to the next annual meeting. Remember, do not share our conversation with anyone."

This plan should be expressed as a strategy for moving from Point A to Point B and how long it should take to get there. The "how to" portion of the strategy should be left to the "experts in their discipline" and their ability to develop the individual strategies to achieve the direction and timeline that have been established. The only real oversight required for this activity is that all within the organization must know the direction. It is important for the leaders of each discipline to understand the overall direction of the company. The direction of each discipline—*and* the company's overall direction—must be known by those responsible for the execution of that strategy. The direction for employee activities that contribute to the achievement of each area's success must be accompanied by a basic understanding of their discipline's total outcome.

### *Organically Grown Through the Generals (Leaders of Each Discipline)*

This form of business development can be difficult to recognize *or* understand. In this business-plan development, middle-level managers and those responsible for leading each discipline have become very in tune with the business's needs and the direction in which it should go. The difficulty in recognizing *why* it has become this way may lead you to two completely opposite conclusions.

The optimistic conclusion of this development method is one where everyone is so in tune with the direction of the company that they are capable of writing the procedures to get there. This requires high employee engagement and motivation to do the right thing for the greater good. *Congratulations!* If you find that your organization is in this state, my only recommendation to you is "keep feeding the beast"! Understand the circumstances that have led you to this state, and continue them. You have the type of organization most leaders will only read and dream about.

The more likely conclusion you may come to is that the leader within each department or discipline must find the need to set the direction for their teams. They do this because they lack a clear understanding of the total organization, or because the one which exists is conflicted and/or confusing. If this is found to be the case, there is inadequate satisfaction that can be derived from the findings. It may still indicate high employee engagement and motivation to do the right thing. It also may not be sustainable without leadership intervention to provide everyone with the basic direction the organization must go and some means of orchestration. Those employees will grow tired of "carrying" the leadership of the organization; they need proper support for their actions.

### There Isn't One

As I mentioned earlier, the condition can exist where a true business plan—the business's driver—has never been created. The company might be on autopilot. **An organization in this state is likely**

**falling behind their competitors and aimed in a direction that is out of date and that has limited relevance when current conditions are considered.** If you find this to be true when completing the assessment, you have two choices: You can quickly run away (not recommended) or recommit yourself to taking back control of the company direction. If you actually have to think about which option is best for you as a leader, it might be time for a new direction in your career . . . sorry for the tough love! One thing you can be assured of is that, if the employees in the organization haven't given up, they will be rooting for you to recommit and lead them through the process. Don't let them down!

## Analyzing Your Assets

The final area of the company self-assessment is to evaluate your business assets. I'm not referring to the assets which historically are closely monitored by companies—that is, those assets which require an initial monetary outlay and have a defined life expectancy. Those are the obvious ones. There are procedures in place in nearly all companies to manage and monitor these types of assets. I want to talk about the less-obvious assets:

**Business Tools:** Let's start by looking at the business tools which enable your employees to do their jobs. Investment in technology and systems are not always looked at in the same way as physical assets that can be seen and touched. They are also not evaluated in the same way. The general rule of thumb for assessing the establishment of new technology in most companies is ROI! If the Return on Investment is slow and inadequate, the new technology won't get approved. This is like operating the business without a business plan.

A comic strip published in *Supply Chain Digest* in December of 2014 sums up many companies' opinions toward the assets I'm suggesting you review.

Investment in the information technology (IT) tools of a company can be nearly as important as the investment in product development and manufacturing equipment. If the general feeling of the organization is that they are not in the business of making things easier for their employees, this not only indicates a shortsighted view of how to promote innovation but also shows a deep disregard for the morale of their employees. Any assessment of your organization's IT product development or purchase should answer the question, "Are we keeping up with today's conditions and properly preparing for future conditions which will influence our business?" If the answer is "No," or you find that your company's approach is like that in the cartoon above, you could be in for some very unpleasant surprises.

**Marketing Tools:** Looking at marketing tools as an asset may seem strange. I'm referring to marketing tools not only at the physical level but also at the intellectual level. A decision to utilize social media to change the marketing direction involves both levels. The purpose for bringing this up as part of the assessment process is to discern if a need exists to innovate or reinvent the process.

Imagine, if, during the time of door-to-door sales of floor-cleaning products, the salespeople didn't adjust their approach on the fly. If the product the salesperson was being directed to push were tools for cleaning bare floors and the salesperson were invited into a house with nothing but carpet, do you think they should try to adjust their approach? If they want to continue to eat, they would. To ensure they are marketing to the appropriate consumer, a business's marketing team (designers, developers, and face-to-face salespeople) must stay current. Just as important, the tools a company uses to evaluate a market must remain up to date and relevant. The ability to gather information on consumers, potential consumers, or lost consumers can make a great foundation for the study of the business tools. The right technology and process to acquire that powerful data is imperative.

**Most Valuable Tools:** Lastly, let's look at the most valuable asset of the organization—its people. The employees of an organization can make it or break it. In like manner, the leadership of an organization can make or break the employees through their actions. Just like a machine operator who misuses equipment entrusted to them, a company leader can shorten and reduce the effectiveness of its employees. It may be hard to view an employee as an "asset" in the same light as a "paid for" asset. An investment in training and education can gradually increase the effectiveness of a new employee—but it should not be a smaller investment than is necessary. Onboarding of a new person has been said to cost as much as $4,000 (not including hiring bonuses and lost productivity during training and maturation of their abilities).

Evaluating a human-being employee is very different from evaluating a machine. You must bring much intuitive analysis to the table in addition to empirical-data analysis. It requires one of the most basic, yet more difficult, assessment methods—listening. Being present with your employees and understanding their needs and conditions is paramount to knowing the general health of these "assets." Periodic employee surveys are a good way to remain aware of their general condition and their attitudes; they also are a great way to gauge if what you are doing to help them is working. Understanding the feedback you get is key to moving the employer-employee relationship forward. This is another time when the worst action you can take is no action. The action you take as a response can create quite an impact on company culture and show your employees that they are valued.

STEP 2

# Understanding the Impact of Culture on the Business

*In this Step:*

- Understanding what a corporate culture is
- Learning how culture impacts motivation
- Adapting the culture to condition changes
- Knowing how deep your culture goes

## WHAT IS CORPORATE CULTURE?

To explain what corporate culture is, I'll first start with what it is not. It is not something defined by the slogans found on the walls of hallways in your building. It is also not the latest Human Resources (HR) training program designed to improve morale or leadership qualifications. If an HR business-plan item becomes "We are going to help them care," you should be looking to re-staff your HR department. This type of approach is like angrily throwing a ball of dried mud against the wall . . . it may make you feel better temporarily, but it isn't going to stick for long. "The beatings will continue until morale improves" has never worked.

> *"Research indicates that workers have three prime needs: Interesting work, recognition for doing a good job, and being let in on things that are going on in the company." —Zig Ziglar*

## HOW A CORPORATE CULTURE IS BEST DEFINED FIRST REQUIRES UNDERSTANDING HOW A CORPORATE CULTURE IS CREATED.

### *The role of the leaders:*

Leaders must embody and model the corporate culture. You may not realize it, but leaders are always being watched. If leaders are lax in how they approach things, it can carry over to the employees. If a leader is passionate and engaged, the employees of the organization are more likely to imitate these characteristics. The concept of "Leadership" must not be limited to the CEO, the President, Vice President, CFO, or COO. Anyone in the organization who manages people (note: I said *manages* and not *leads* for a reason) is a leader. The "Middle Management" of an organization will likely have a bigger influence on how a corporate culture evolves than the top rungs on the corporate ladder. They are seen, heard, and observed more often because of their daily, almost constant, interaction with the employees. Still, they may be less likely to understand the role they play in shaping the culture. If leaders "in the trenches" with the employees of the organization choose to complain, even if they think they are representing the opinions of their direct-report employees, they are, unwittingly, doing them a disservice. A better approach is to listen empathetically to them and provide them with guidance and reasoning (not excuses or "washing their hands of the situation").

### The company's actions:

A corporate culture is also driven by the "deeds" of the organization and its individuals. The deeds of the organization are, in turn, driven by what is demonstrated as being important in the organization.

If the organization is driven by money (which one isn't?), the deeds can start to move away from the culture most companies want to establish. Take Wells Fargo, for example. Everyone knows their story and how employees were incentivized through compensation or punishment (as stated in a *New York Times* article by Emily Flitter and Stacy Cowley, published January 23, 2020) to achieve established quotas. As quotas were achieved, they were increased (raising the bar). Employees who tended to be resourceful and understood what was expected of them began taking measures to achieve those quotas. They reportedly began pushing products to customers that weren't needed or wanted and, as indicated in the article, "bending or breaking internal rules to meet ambitious performance goals." Ask yourself: Is this the type of behavior you would encourage within your own organization? Have you? Is this the type of behavior you would like to be known for personally? If you answered "Yes," the rest of this book's content is not for you unless you are open to an intervention of sorts. Let me ask the same question from a different perspective: Is this the type of company you would do business with if you were receiving that type of service? It is never too late to change!

The reason this example is important goes back to my earlier statement about the company culture not being contained in the slogans on the wall. The message this may have conveyed to their employees went something like: "Meet Your Goals at All Costs!" or "The Customer Doesn't Know What They Need. Upsell!" The hallway walls there were likely more "talk" and less "walk."

As the article represents, the outcome of these deeds became the culture by which Wells Fargo reportedly did business. It cost them monetarily ("more than $1.5 billion in federal- and state-authority levied fines" as well as "$620 million to resolve lawsuits from customers and shareholders"). It cost them reputationally, and it most likely cost them customers. Now, quite a bit of time is being taken for "apologizing" for their actions and trying to prove they have changed in order to win back customers. It takes a complete overhaul of the corporate culture and some really good leadership to make those actions be seen, heard, and felt. As they are a long-standing company, I hope they achieve that success.

> *"Always treat your employees exactly as you want them to treat your best customers."—Stephen R. Covey*

### The attitude of the team:

Lastly, a corporate culture is formed by a feeling. The first two drivers focused more on what you can see. This driver is different. Walking into an office or any work environment for the first time can reveal a lot to you about a company. Have you ever been to an office where, when a leader enters a workroom, all eyes raise from their work with an uneasy look? I have! That first observation can lead you to a couple of different conclusions. These people are not really busy and looking for a diversion to take up a little bit of their day—or they are scared to death about who might be coming into their area. I'm not saying it is a bad thing for everyone to want to know who just came into their environment, but wouldn't we all want to see them giving you a look like "This might be a potential customer or someone I might want to know"? Don't even think about trying to force it, because it will be obvious.

Likewise, walking into a manufacturing environment can be very telling. I have entered that type of environment with a very well-meaning owner and could immediately see how his employees responded to his presence. They were trying to look busy and/or hiding something they were doing that was against policy. What that told me is that they were motivated by fear and not respect. They were just doing a job. As soon as a better one presented itself, they would be gone!

The other way you can get a feel for what a corporate culture is in an organization is simply to *listen*. You can't force caring. You can't force passion. You can't force excitement. These are all emotions which will naturally come through in a discussion about the business and about the contributions each person can make to it. I have found active, genuine *listening* to be one of the most effective ways to gain insight into a company. Quotas might spark excitement, but if the method by which they are attained does not make you feel good about it personally, it will taint the excitement. It is going to show through.

One caution for the observer: Don't let the experience of a single "bad day" diminish your assessment of the level of excitement—don't let "one bad day" leave you with the belief it is a "bad culture." It might be possible to temporarily suppress excitement, but true passion and caring will ultimately show through. I can cite numerous occasions while conducting interviews for potential employees where it was tough to reflect true excitement for being a part of the company I was representing. Have you ever been required to "interrupt" a really challenging day to go meet with a young person fresh out of college, interviewing for their first professional job? I nearly always found that having the conversation with them and explaining about the company and what my role in it was had an almost *therapeutic* effect on me. It reminded me how that bad day really didn't spoil the true passion I had for the company, and the interviewee would walk away knowing it would be a good company to work for. True and genuine passion can't be suppressed. It takes only a couple of probing questions to bring it out.

## CULTURAL IMPACT ON MOTIVATION

### *Culture of Money*

I want to share some observations I have made over the years on the impact a culture can have on its employees. The Wells Fargo culture was a "Culture of Money," which is more susceptible to outside influences such as recessions or market downturns. It is not the type of culture most people would choose to participate in. Not that their bottom line might be any more affected than another company's, but the response and subsequent actions likely will be. As I mentioned in Step 1, this is like building your foundation in the sand.

A company that finds itself in this situation is likely to react (or overreact) to the conditions with an intent to "turn things around." No one can stop a storm when it comes up; all you can do is weather it. Would you try to stop a hurricane, or would you try to prepare yourself for it? With the sole focus on the bottom line, actions will be altered in order to continue to achieve the desired outcome. An organization without a sound culture may resort to short-term cost cutting, which impacts longer-term company health and competitiveness. Taking the focus off the customer can lead to the potential loss of current or future customers; staffing decisions focused on the bottom line will result in the loss of high performers. Those lost employees are the ones who have the potential to lead the recovery when conditions improve. Without loyal customers sticking by your side during a time of challenge, you may not have a business when that improvement comes. Messaging for employees can become very ambiguous when they are told they have to sacrifice because of the business conditions, yet the profit and performance of the organization do not reflect it . . . *in the short term.*

I would liken this last example to the difficult times endured during the 2007-2008 global financial crisis deemed "The Great Recession." At that time, I addressed a group of transportation providers and delivered a very somber message to let them know what they could expect. I also delivered a message of hope, along with my personal expectations. Many companies at that time were locking up the safe and eliminating spending. My message of hope and expectation to them was this: "We are entering a very foggy period. When we emerge from the fog, we are going to want to run with the pedal to the floorboard to make up for lost time. Now is not a time to relax or withdraw. This time should be used to assess yourselves and determine how you can be a better company when we all emerge, and be prepared to keep pace." Many of those companies took that message to heart and expressed their appreciation later for providing them a small ray of hope and direction at a time which looked pretty dire.

### Culture of People

Now let's discuss a completely different approach, a "Culture of People." This culture is focused more on "Do the right thing, and the results will come." The act of doing the right thing can and will motivate employees and bring greater engagement. Human nature drives people toward a sense of belonging. This means not only belonging from a contribution standpoint but also being a part of something great. I've seen this type of environment where excitement over new products and new benefits emerges and takes the focus off of targets and rules. The employees become engaged and stay engaged through the genuine excitement they can see in the management team. Remember, they are always watching.

A company which operates on an ethical, empathetic, and encouraging business model is one an employee can get behind and feel good about. Of course, that can't be sustained if results aren't delivered. If the product is good, if business methods are focused on the customer, and if people are engaged, the chances for success are extremely high.

The reason for bringing this contrast in business approaches to light should be pretty evident by now. While you were reading the past several paragraphs, hopefully, you were comparing and contrasting which type of company environment you could function in best. With only a few exceptions, I have to believe everyone would choose a "Culture of People" company to establish their career with.

Unfortunately, when you're job-hunting, the true culture of an organization doesn't always present itself in an interview or meeting with other employees of the company. From my personal experience interviewing more candidates than I can possibly remember, nearly all walked away stating they could tell it would be a good place to work. It can take years of developing the assessment skills to make that determination if the interviewer isn't transparent. And it is possible for the culture to change after you make the decision to join a company.

### *"Run, Hide, Fight"*

If you find yourself immersed in a toxic environment, it doesn't mean all is lost. There are multiple options still open to you. If you have ever taken active-shooter training, you know that they teach "Run, Hide, Fight" as your options. Similarly, when you find yourself in a company which isn't what you had hoped for, and their culture doesn't align with your own beliefs, you still have options. You can Run ... and look for another company which better fits your beliefs; you can Hide ... lie low, make your contributions, and view the job as just that, a job; you can Fight ... to change a corporate culture. Changing corporate culture can come from any direction. If you have it in you to be the catalyst to reinvent the culture of the company you are in, by all means, *do it*! Be ready for a potentially long journey with a potential for personal satisfaction at the end that can be amazing. You might even find there are others who would like to join in the fight! Be realistic, though. Changing a company's culture by yourself, from the ground up, doesn't always work, and you may have to derive your satisfaction from knowing you tried. Regardless of the outcome, my opinion is that the journey is always worth it!

## ALIGNING THE CULTURE TO THE CONDITIONS

Unless you are an incredible recruiter and prolific at picking the right candidates for your team, you could find yourself in very different conditions over time. Prevailing conditions can change. The very best team may find themselves up against formidable conditions, and they can become a struggling team. Situational-leadership skills must be used for adapting your approach and leadership style (one of the key components that impact your company culture), to ensure that you survive. This can hold true also with your own, personal life. Here are some examples:

**Example 1:** You, as a leader, have a very talented and creative team. They are the type of "autopilot" team that you can provide with a general definition of where you want to go, minimal rules for getting there, and the scantest of resources to make the journey with—and they will achieve the outcome you want. Congratulations! Turn them loose, and watch what they can do. If your team fits this definition, they will likely thrive and bring some amazing opportunities your way.

Until the situation changes.

**Example 2:** You are leading in a new area you have just established, with a mix of experienced and new team members. New to the company, new to the process—what can possibly go wrong, right? The leadership style must be very different in this situation. Hands-on leadership, with a lot of oversight, is a must. Jumping in and doing the process side by side and teaching as you go is probably the approach that is required. This is the best way to show your team you are vested in their success and willing to do everything to become successful together.

Where situational leadership comes in is when you recognize that the conditions are no longer suitable for you to lead your people as you historically have. When a creative team is not able to apply their capability due to a lack of funding or a lack of customer demand, which slows everything down, it is not possible to interact with them the same way. More guidance and oversight will be required to keep them focused on relevant issues and opportunities.

Likewise, there are opportunities where your staff may be highly internally motivated. If you apply the same, continued level of oversight described above, it might make them feel like you don't trust them and just want to nag. Finding the right balance and understanding when and how to change your approach is as much an art as it is a science. Sticking with the same approach without recognizing that a change in conditions has taken place can be damaging to the morale of the parties you are leading and an impediment to the type of culture you are attempting to build.

The best method I have found is to apply both approaches—let the team operate creatively and independently, and, when changes in the conditions dictate, tighten up the control a little. Once you have developed this skill, you have put a really powerful tool into your tool belt. Make sure you use it and continue to hone it. If you don't have it, work hard to get it. Your company, employees, and family will appreciate it more than you can imagine.

Finally, because your approach can be construed as inconsistent or unpredictable by many, it is always best to "keep it real." Clearly communicating the change in approach is the best method to avoid any confusion or wrong observations. If the team understands you are becoming more involved because the conditions dictate—not because they have lost your trust—they are more likely to embrace the change. In the home environment, as long as your child(ren) know(s) you are now watching their actions more closely because of a change in conditions, they are less likely to think the change is because you feel like they can't be independent. Simple communication can go a long way in both environments, but many don't find communication so simple. Of course, for those of us who have been both children and parents, we know that all these rules go out the window at about age fourteen, right?

## THE DEEP ROOTS OF CULTURE

Now you might be thinking, *Is this entire book going to be about culture?* The answer is "No" . . . "Yes" . . . "Maybe." It is important that a company culture shapes just about everything you do, how you do it, and how the company is perceived. It is the definition of what your company objectives state and how your company mission statement is shaped. It really is that important, in my view; it establishes some deep roots and a strong foundation on which you can build an amazing structure. Or it can be a very shaky one if done wrong.

Imagine that, as a consumer, you walk into a business and see a company mission statement that goes something like this: "Through All Means Necessary, We Will Sell Our Products to More Customers at a Greater Profit to Support Our Bottom Line." Ridiculous as it may seem, a bad company culture can take a well-intentioned mission statement and turn the results into a ridiculous outcome.

Through a strong and ethical company culture, endurability for the business can be established. The mission statement can become one that defines why your business exists, how you intend to conduct it, and how you hope to be perceived by the community at large. "Being a Good Corporate Citizen" is a statement made by nearly every company that provides a product or service to the community. Those with a strong and ethical culture will be the organizations which actually make it happen. Commitment to Quality, commitment to Value, and commitment to the Customer will shine through and become a basic tenet of the organization.

Companies can also go through a state of "flux" when it comes to their culture. Changes in conditions, changes in leadership, and changes in competition can push a company away from their original beliefs . . . whether it is recognized or not. I'll go into much greater detail about a changing culture during the next step, so I'll refrain from further explanation about a culture shift here. But I do want to offer that you should never underestimate the need to nurture your organization's culture once you've built the right one.

Lastly, I'd like to share views of how a negative culture can contribute to the demise of a company. This explanation is not postulated on an actual company that was taken down by a bad culture—although I'm sure if you have been in business for very long, you can probably come up with some examples on your own. My intent with this section is to outline what "can" happen when a bad culture or lack of culture influences a company and ultimately leads to its demise. Hopefully, this content will provide some warning signs that you can use to identify when conditions arise in your environment, or maybe they already exist.

Which best represents your company culture by action?

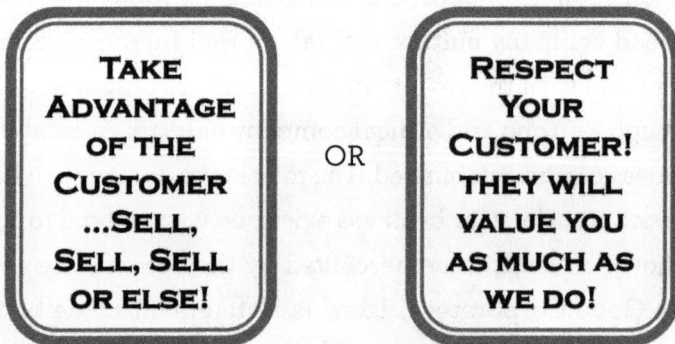

| **TAKE ADVANTAGE OF THE CUSTOMER ...SELL, SELL, SELL OR ELSE!** | OR | **RESPECT YOUR CUSTOMER! THEY WILL VALUE YOU AS MUCH AS WE DO!** |

While these examples seem a little bit inane as bulletin-board material, you get the picture. And remember, they are intended to represent your actions and not your published mission statement!

There are several warning signs, not visible to the eye, which might tip you off that a negative culture is already at work in destroying your company. Some of these signs may also be present in and apply to your home environment.

Here are some of those signs:

> ➤ Member disengagement: This can describe everything from an employee, a manager, a spouse, or a child who may no longer want to participate in the activities of the group. For an organization, this may result in high turnover and/or sudden or early retirement in order to leave the toxic environment. The loss of those members can be disturbing for the organization. If it is truly an indication of a bad environment, it is nearly as important to understand why the others stayed. That is especially true if the higher performers are among those who leave.

> ➤ Loss in productivity: This can manifest itself in two ways. It can be seen as an unexplained reduction in output or a sudden increase in production problems and equipment malfunctions (in a manufacturing environment). This can also originate from an increased absence of employees who do so within the rules of the organization (medical leave, family leave, sick days, etc.).

> ➤ Loss of communication: Problems which go unreported until they are a big issue can start to occur. Communication within the management organization can start to degrade. Communication within the employees can start to degrade. Open lines of communication between employees and management become a complaint line directly to Human Resources, outside public or media. While communication between the

employees and HR should never be discouraged, when this becomes the only line of communication between the employee and management, it is less healthy.

These are just a few of the most telling signs that a culture within an organization may not be promoting the best way of doing business. They all say to an informed observer that a lack of trust and civility exists in the organization. I'll go into more of this analysis in later steps.

*"Appreciate everything your associates do for the business. Nothing else can quite substitute for a few well-chosen, well-timed, sincere words of praise. They're absolutely free and worth a fortune."* —Sam Walton

◖

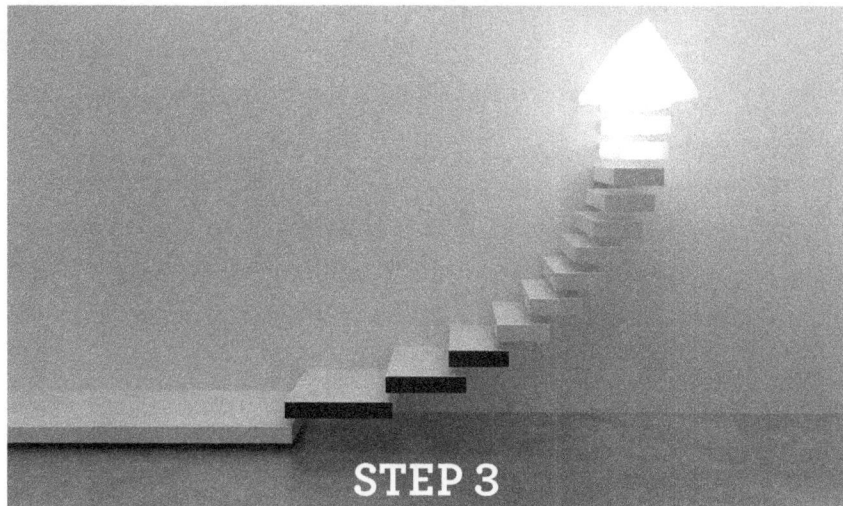

## STEP 3

# Recognizing That the Culture Is Changing

*In this Step:*

- Understanding and recognizing destruction of the culture
- Discovering the visible signs
- Watching out for forced caring

## DESTRUCTION OF THE CULTURE

In this step, I hope to help you understand and recognize when a culture is changing in an organization, a team, or even a family if you are looking at it from that perspective. Sometimes a change can be so subtle that it goes unnoticed. If you have ever visited with a friend or relative you don't see very often with your child, you might hear the statement, "Oh, my, you have grown a foot." Then you realize your friend or relative who isn't around your child every day can see how much change has taken place, where you may not. Because you see them every day, the change is so subtle, you don't even notice it . . . apart from continuously growing food, clothing, and shoe bills.

In a business environment, the same thing can happen to you. A change in an employee's actions or attitude happens, and you pass it off as an anomaly. Then it begins to happen more frequently, and you might call it an 'anormally'. Then it becomes the norm! You have just been guided through how a culture shift occurs in 50 words or less. It sometimes seems it can happen just that fast. It is much like erosion, and, unless you have markers in place to detect it and address it, it will happen to you.

Let's talk first about where the destruction of a company culture can originate from (the implication here is that the change is one that is not welcome). As you will see from these explanations, it can come from a number of sources, and some might be surprising. I genuinely hope that, as you read, you will ask yourself, "Am I the cause?" Sometimes the actions of one person can be the leading contributor. The attitudes or mannerisms of a single individual begin to rub off on the whole team if not caught early.

Here are some of the key drivers for a negative change to a company culture as I see them:

**Leadership Factor:** If you are someone responsible for leading any type of team, regardless how large or how small, this is where you should become very introspective. I realize asking that of you is not an overly nice thing to do to someone, but it is totally necessary to become a better person and a better leader.

When I say that a negative cultural impact can be leadership-driven, I'm not talking about a purposeful, deliberate dismantling of a company's culture . . . although some individuals will embark on that endeavor. I'm talking about actions that often have negative unintended consequences. These actions may go unnoticed by everyone, including the one creating them, but are certainly felt. In the next Step, I'll go into several ways a leader can create an environment where a negative impact can be seen . . . but please don't read ahead! I hope everything covered in this Step will give a good foundation for that next discussion.

In an organization of any type or size, there will always be good and bad leaders. A bad leader can become a good leader or even a great leader with the right amount of training and development . . . if they can listen with sincerity. I would also caution that a "good leader" can become a bad one if their continuous development is ignored. If you encounter a "bad leader"—one who consistently displays a total lack of sincerity in their ability to listen, change, or move away from a hubris created by the feeling they are always right and/or it is someone else's problem when things go wrong—remove them immediately from their position. Either way, the negative effect that comes with bad leadership must be stopped! Reform or remove. This may seem harsh, but instead of the risk of further damage to the organization and trust among the employees, it is a necessary action. If, during your analysis, you find *you* are the leader creating those unintended consequences . . . *get help now!*

> *"Leaders who don't listen will eventually be surrounded by people who have nothing to say"* —Andy Stanley

**Organic Factor:** This condition can be difficult to assess and resolve. In Step 2, I discussed adapting the approach taken when dealing with employees or children when conditions change. The same holds true with assigning the right people to the task at hand. What is meant by an "Organic" driver is that the alignment of people to what is taking place at the time can be all wrong if you don't continually assess where you are in the journey. Having the wrong person in the wrong role at the wrong time can be disastrous . . . to both the outcome and the person's self-confidence.

Let's say you were traveling around the world. In order to experience different parts of the countryside as well as remote ports of call, you decide the best mode of transport is multiple modes of transport (air, ground, and water). While you are traveling the ocean by ship, you have the best ship captain one could ever hope for. They navigate the storms perfectly, make additional stops in order for you to experience islands where no other mode of transport can afford to go, and make the trip perfect! Once you make your final port, the next transit mode is by air. The ship captain was so good that you ask them to bring their crew and pilot your aircraft. I know, ridiculous! But that is exactly my point. Adapting the team to changing conditions is one of the most important things a leader can do. That's not to say you let everyone go and start all over—you change the formula of the team and ensure you have the right makeup for the conditions and the right "Captain" for the next mode of business.

**"Where did they put the helm?"**

Failing to identify these needs can change the performance, change the emotional state of the employees, lead to a lack of trust in the leadership and create a negative impact to the overall culture of the organization. That is why this condition is one that is very difficult to recognize as impacting company culture, but it still has a major impact on it.

**Goal Factor:** Do not misconstrue this as a belief that goals should be abandoned. Quite the contrary . . . they should be established with a deep commitment from everyone in the organization to understand their importance and to work toward achieving them. The goals of an organization can have a negative impact on culture when those goals stand in contrast to what is believed to be right by those who are assigned to ensure the goals are met. This is a point where every employee, no matter their position in the organization, reaches the "Run, Hide, Fight" decision in their career.

From the standpoint of a large organization, we need to look no further than the example of Wells Fargo, which I mentioned earlier. That is where the goals of the organization likely didn't match the beliefs of many of their employees. Without statistics to back it up, I can't say there were those who stood on their beliefs and determined that was not an organization they wanted to work for, but it would make sense. Those with strong core beliefs who stayed either sacrificed those beliefs or were blind to what was really happening.

In a small organization, as with many of the other conditions I have and will mention, the impact may be seen much faster and will likely be much more stronger. As I stated earlier, an individual's choices come down to *run, hide,* or *fight.* In a smaller organization, where it is more likely there is not a reporting structure to register a complaint or comment unless it is to the owner, *run* or *hide* becomes the more likely choice. Leaving the organization (*run*) is the moral high ground, but staying and performing your duties (*hide*) cannot be construed as sacrificing one's personal beliefs. After all, I believe we have all been caught up in a condition where we are not in our "forever job," and we know it ... but we still need it. Those growing children still need shoes, right?

In a larger organization, there is still opportunity to attempt to enact change (*fight*). Since most employees are far removed from the owners, board of directors, or CEOs, the opportunity to bring those changes using the reporting structures is not in place. More opportunities exist to share the ideas you hope will achieve the desired outcome but may require using a different approach. Bringing those alternative options which do not work against what the company stands for or stand in contrast to the desired goals can create a grass-roots movement within the company. Similar to my statement about negative culture impacting attitudes, or mannerisms rubbing off on others, a positive approach to achieve company objectives can rub off on the entire organization as well. As stated earlier, be prepared for a battle that could deliver some serious frustration and/or some amazing satisfaction.

**Communication Gap Factor:** This can be tricky to identify as well. It would be easy to recognize this as conflicting goals, as defined above, because the goals may not be known by anyone but the person developing them. This is something that can easily become the case in a small business and, fortunately, can also be easily remedied. In a large organization, as I discussed in Step One, this can still happen where the business plan and expected goals are not known by those who should be making them happen—or perhaps have not been established at all.

In any organization, this can become an issue caused by bad (or no) messaging. Even if a business plan is established in an organization, if it is left open to interpretation, with ambiguous goals, the message which reaches those responsible for its execution can become diluted, changed, or lost in translation. This, too, can happen in virtually any size of organization where the top leadership may share his or her vision of where the organization should go with the management members responsible for diffusing it to the masses, and the approach or objective is "interpreted" prior to it being shared.

One example is the age-old game of "telephone." A line or circle of people is created with the intention of passing along a message by whispering it to the next person from the beginning of the line to the last person in line. The message is passed from each person to the next by repeating the original message, verbatim. The goal is to have the message or action be the same when the last person conveys it as it was when the first person delivered it. We all know how that goes, don't we? Only through that process can a statement as simple as "red raspberries are sweet" become "cherries are on the street." Okay, silly example—but you get the picture: An intended goal to be shared with the entire organization can certainly lose its urgency and priority within the company. It can also happen that the approach becomes so adjusted based on the manager's own agenda that the original goals can't be achieved. Clear communication from the leader/originator to all parties in the organization is a way to ensure checks and balances exist.

**Reward Factor:** This type of issue can also be created by the leadership of the organization. One way it manifests itself is through rewarding the wrong behaviors. Too often, leaders will misinterpret someone's contributions and, for the wrong reasons, promote the wrong people into the wrong positions because they see more in them than really exists. I'll go further into the characteristics of some of these employees in the next Step to outline what you should watch for. For this discussion, let's just say that, often, an employee will be recognized because they talk about things that happen but are, in fact, not involved in any of it happening. These "talkers" are seen as being intelligent as opposed to just informed. And many times, rewards are handed out for those focusing on the short-term gain of the company while not contributing to the long-term benefits. This happens when someone knows the topical facts but does not know what the facts really entail.

Why is this so damaging? When employees see the wrong people being rewarded with promotions, raises (yeah, they talk), or key assignments, the demoralizing effects will become rapidly known. As an employee, you have two recourses. One, you learn to play the game. This may result in a dramatic reduction in productivity (yours and the company's) or in a degradation of morale. Playing the game entails listening to those employees who are creating, resolving, inventing, or formulating their own theses and sharing them. The more people who see this as a method of advancing, the fewer employees there are actually creating, resolving, or inventing. The second choice is for you to go somewhere else, where you can be recognized for true contributions; this will also result in reduced productivity within the current organization. Either way, the entire organization suffers from unintended consequences brought about by an action which may have originally been thought of as being a positive.

The other Reward Driven consequence can be brought about by not recognizing someone's positive action or result. Personally, I have always been motivated by accomplishment. That meant that, when I completed something, the last thing on my mind was celebrating the accomplishment just experienced. I wanted to get on to the next conquest while the adrenaline rush was still present. Remember ... success begets success? In contrast to my personality, I was once told by a very wise person: "Take time to celebrate." Under-rewarding a person or group of individuals who have just achieved a significant accomplishment can also have some unintended consequences . . . the feeling of being underappreciated. Don't get caught in this trap. In a small organization, showing appreciation and recognizing accomplishments can be something as simple as a lunch for everyone. It could also be something more substantial, such as a small bonus if the financial impact is large. In a larger organization, it can be recognition in a company newsletter or a team event. Regardless of how small the gesture seems, it is a positive way to show appreciation and avoid a negative result. Be cautious not to overdo the recognition and dilute the effect. Participation trophies in business can be quite damaging.

## THE VISIBLE SIGNS

Let's talk a little bit about the visible signs your company culture is changing. I've already mentioned some of the key drivers that might prompt a change to your company culture. As mentioned, some of those changes can be quite subtle, since you are immersed in it every day. You may not notice that your employees are becoming less and less excited about coming to work. You may not notice that your thirteen-year-old child's attitude is becoming more and more combative and disrespectful. And then one day you realize that everything has changed. You have to be aware of the signs as they are building. Catching the signs earlier may help avoid the issues later.

There are the obvious signs. Even though I'm calling them "obvious," sometimes they aren't. They are obvious if you monitor statistics or take the time to pay attention and listen. Within a small-business environment, there are some factors that stand out quite prevalently.

### Obvious Signs

An example of that would be employee turnover. It is much more noticeable in an office of 10 people as opposed to a company of

10,000. The result is likely to be a loss that most companies can't afford to have as business conditions become more complex . . . does it ever get easier? Turnover in our current environment can be even more impactful, since recruiting and bringing on qualified replacements is more difficult. You don't need a statistician to tell you there is a disturbing turnover trend when you are having to replace two desk nameplates every month. Statistics can be quite useful in a larger company to help understand why the turnover rates are accelerating. This type of information is usually compiled by your HR Department.

The unfortunate trend I have seen and heard is that not enough emphasis has been placed on the "exit interview" to collect the true, root cause of employees leaving. Not asking the probing questions to ensure they are learning the honest reason for an employee leaving the organization is a disservice and doesn't build the data necessary to address the conditions causing the turnover issue. That should be a key . . . I said *key* . . . responsibility and expectation of every HR Department. If you want *No* issues, then *Know* the issues, and fix them. I understand that asking the difficult questions and listening to the truth in return may be quite uncomfortable. Too often, I believe HR Departments don't want to be the bearer of bad news and might ignore trends.

Other more subtle but still obvious signs require a bit more intuitive data gathering (not factual data gathering). They can be employee malaise and working less (hard) enthusiastically. I left my adjustment in wording in the content as a hidden meaning. My original thought was the employee just isn't going to work as hard anymore. That might be a bit harsh and sound like a purposeful slowdown on their part. I didn't want to make it sound that way . . . even though it is the result. The employee might not even realize they aren't working as hard. They just don't have the same type of enthusiasm they may have once had. The best way to see this type of result taking place is by paying closer attention (therefore, intuitive). Employees extending breaks or lunches, taking more personal time during the day, coming in late, leaving early—these are all possible signs that the enthusiasm is waning. It can also be signs of conditions impacting the employee outside the work environment, but that will tend to be individualized and not a general condition of all employees. Once again, early detection when the signs start to appear makes improving the conditions much easier.

### Subtle Signs

There are also subtle signs. If the enthusiasm has begun to wane, there can be signs which indicate your employees are starting to view their position with the company as "just a job." It can manifest itself in some of the obvious signs (if you are paying attention), when you see employees (especially salaried) coming in late (or exactly on time) and leaving early (or exactly on time) all the time. This is a good indication they have lost the enthusiasm to always do everything they can to advance their career. It's not a career anymore . . . it's "just a job."

### Hidden, Visible Signs

And lastly, there are the hidden, yet visible signs. Does that sound not quite right to you? You probably have me on that one. These signs are visible, but you must look closely, or, in some cases, feel them. A sign that would be hidden, yet visible would be when innovation in the company starts to slow to a crawl or stop altogether. This happens when there isn't anyone with enough experience or motivation to tackle the hard stuff. It can begin as apathy by some, which results in fewer and fewer employees who will accept the hard or nearly impossible assignments and who are excited to tackle them. Then over time, the apathy spreads as those few dedicated employees remaining to tackle the hard stuff, start to get tired, and see that everything gets put on their shoulders. Before you know it, there is nobody willing to pick up the ball and run with it. Either the leaders start doing everything, or, worse, game over!

The good news, as I have stated throughout this Step, if detected early, the opportunity will usually exist to right the ship before it is too late.

## FORCED CARING—THE NEXT "HR" PROGRAM

OK, so someone has identified that your organization has lost the foundation it was established on. The culture has changed, and you know it! What do you do? The easiest action is no action at all—just like ignoring a cracking and crumbling foundation in your home. Maybe it will go away or heal itself. Please be sure to let me know how that goes. I may be in the market for a vacant lot to build on. Likewise, no action is the easiest action for the business you have established and worked hard to build. I don't believe you would be willing to watch that business crumble and no longer exist.

Another approach is to establish a new Human Resources program—we'll call it HRP, since all businesses love acronyms! The new HRP will be designed to help the employees understand why they should want to try harder, participate, and be involved in bettering the company. After all, it is not only their right but their responsibility. Let's call our new HRP "CREAM." This will stand for "Cultural Renovation Through Employee Action and Morale." The goal of this new program is to inspire all of our employees to care again by "CREAMing" them. They will be "CREAMed" in the art of applying themselves more. They will be "CREAMed" in the new programs we are going to launch that can provide recognition incentives if they go above and beyond. We are going to demonstrate to our employees the benefits of caring more!

**If you read that last paragraph and thought it sounded like a reasonable strategy, something is *seriously wrong with you!* It is**

**intended to: #1 make you laugh through the use of sarcasm and #2 demonstrate just how inane some ideas can be.** There are, of course, no bad ideas, just some that are less thought through than others. And some are better brought to fruition than others, at least in their beginning forms.

If it sounds as if I am a complete opponent of HR organizations, I'm not. Some of my favorite people in the organizations I've worked in have been those I have worked with in the HR operations. But, understand their role in the organization. You wouldn't (or shouldn't) ask your accounting organization to lead your manufacturing operations. You wouldn't (or shouldn't) ask your manufacturing operations' leaders to manage your financials. Likewise, don't ask your HR organization to create the best method to motivate your employees. The best and most equipped people to do that are the leaders who manage, interact with, and listen to the employees every single day. An organically grown approach will always be better and on the mark to address the most pressing issues as seen from the employees' viewpoint.

If you do, in fact, decide to ask your HR professionals to lead your "Cultural Renovation," be cautious that an Employee Propagandization doesn't occur. The tendency would be to establish a "marketing blitz" with posters, newsletters, stickers, magnets, pens, etc., which contain your new "CREAM" logo. As I mentioned before, if the actions of leaders don't match expectations being placed on your employees, the HRP might as well be titled "TNT" instead of "CREAM." It will blow up in your face pretty quickly. The employees will take a dismissive attitude toward the program as being just another way to try to make them care. In the end, you can't teach caring, but you can nurture it—if it exists and it is not too late!

Incentivizing the actions taken by employees is one way to promote the results you are looking for. This, too, can become a short-lived burst of adrenaline. If not properly directed at solving the employees' lack of action and undesired attitudes, achieving the result of turning around the company culture will become just another program. It then becomes another expected part of the compensation package through the completion of another task. It will be seen as just another job.

If you have ever, as a parent, increased your child's allowance for taking on additional tasks around the house to help the family, you understand how my "short-lived" reference manifests itself. Initially, when more money comes into play, doing the extra work is the means to reach the end. There is a short-term adrenaline burst, and they are happy to do the extra work. Over time, the honeymoon ends, and they decide "The extra incentive isn't worth the extra work . . . and besides, maybe Mom and/or Dad won't realize they are still paying me, even if I stopped doing the work." The child who will continue to do the extra work is the one who recognizes their contribution to the family and truly cares about making that contribution. The same holds true with employees. If they care, they will do the extra work because it is the right thing to do and because it gives them a sense of contributing to something greater than just themselves.

The employees who truly care and want to do the right thing are the type of people you want in your organization. Surrounding yourself with them is a very smart thing to do, but it's not easy. It was always a goal of mine, and I can honestly state I had some good success with it. That is why I was able to accomplish things greater than I ever believed possible . . . through (with) them and their hard work and dedication!

❍

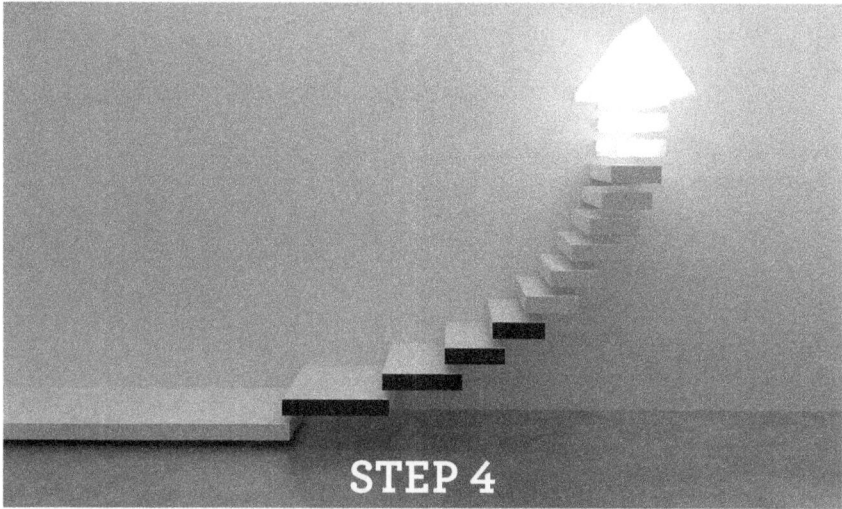

## STEP 4

# When the Personnel Pool
# Becomes Polluted

*In this Step:*
- Assessing the pollution in the personnel pool
- Identifying what can pollute the personnel pool
- Determining if conflict is scaring everyone away

### Polluting the Waters . . . Multiple Ways

Despite the continuous hard work to build the perfect team of only the best and brightest employees, sometimes the "Personnel Pool" can become polluted. In this section, I want to touch on how that happens and what (who) the pollutants are. There are some key areas which might come as a bit of a surprise to you that can have a big impact on what and who can change the "pH" level of an organization.

The three main polluting actions I want to discuss are:

> **Attrition**

> **Promotion**

> **Hiring**

**Attrition:** As you gain ground on your efforts to build the best team possible, any influence which starts an exodus from the organization can have a profound impact on the team (pH) balance. Think back on times when you played on the playground when you were a young child. If there was a see-saw or teeter-totter or whatever you may have called it in your area of the country, maybe you remember how important it was to get a good balance on the board to make it work properly. Moving the board on the fulcrum could make up for having a person or people on the two ends who didn't match in weight. If someone suddenly jumped off the board once you got the right balance, the results weren't what you wanted . . . and probably hurt!

That attrition from the see-saw board is very similar to the outcome which can be experienced in the business environment. As mentioned in the last Step, if it is a small business, it can be felt immediately and dramatically. In a larger business, it may take a little longer. If the attrition is of like-minded people, it is likely you have many of the same types of employees leaving for the same reason or new opportunity. This is similar to the effect of everybody on one side of the see-saw board jumping off at the same time. Regardless of the size of your organization, attrition can be felt from both a productivity and a financial standpoint.

Attrition is not always the result of something bad. It can be driven by the fact that employee development in an organization becomes notably something special. Sometimes, as you create super employees, they become very desirable to the competition—or even other areas within your own organization. You can find consolation in the fact you are great at developing people, but it still hurts! The good news is that word spreads, and there will be good people who want to better themselves and are dying to be a part of your organization, so the recruitment pool available to fill the open positions will be good. Think about this condition as it exists in the best college sports teams. The best athletes beat those universities' doors down to be a part of that team. Knowing there is a high likelihood they will be at that university for only one to two years as a steppingstone to a professional contract, the athlete, the coaches, and the university all plan for that. You hear of those schools "reloading" with new talent, and they generally don't miss a beat.

The attrition you should be more concerned with is when good talent is leaving for the wrong reasons. Whether it is because of competitive pay, available benefits, or leadership and cultural differences, it is a condition which needs to be addressed. So, you ask, how does that attrition impact the pH balance in the workforce? Generally, it means that the talent level is going to be diminished. Those left in the organization become the employees who are less likely to be able to better their employment condition by leaving, so they stay. Of course, that is not the case with everyone. The exception will be those who maintain a loyalty to the organization or a leader, regardless of the circumstances. Those who remain become your future leaders by default, and the organization may have had to settle for less. I know that is a harsh statement, but it is true. That isn't to say the employees can't develop into good leaders; it just might take more time and, likely, more effort to make that happen. If the cause of the attrition is the leadership, who is going to teach them?

**Promotion:** That leads us into the next section of what might cause the Polluted Personnel Pool (say that ten times fast without spraying everyone around you . . . in a COVID-19 environment you might need to double-mask). Once an organization starts promoting employees who are not the best but the best who are left, it can have an avalanche effect. A less-qualified person takes a leadership position, where they are mentored by an unqualified leader. The result is likely going to be a bad situation... but not always. Sometimes a diamond in the rough exists, and a person becomes a leader they would want to work for instead of a leader they currently work for. Not great odds, but it can happen. By contrast, if you put those same people in an organization with good leadership and solid mentoring, that "diamond" gets polished quicker.

In the last Step, I talked about how rewarding wrong behaviors can have a negative effect on a company culture. This "settle for" cycle is a good example of that. Someone is promoted not because they are qualified but because they are the most qualified person we have. Good for them, bad for the organization. Honestly, it is good for them for only a limited time. If the new leader doesn't burn out, they will be the most likely to burn bridges and may find themselves in a short-term position and disillusioned with the company. That person's confidence is likely to get shaken, and it is very possible they will regress back into a so-so employee.

**Hiring:** You might think this pollutant is related to hiring the wrong people or not hiring the right people to join your team. In a way it is, but I want to apply a twist. What I want to primarily focus on is *wrongly hiring who you think are the right people*. Take a second for that settle in ....

If you have ever seen the *Austin Powers* movies, you are probably familiar with the character Dr. Evil. His approach was to surround himself with like-minded people. That desire was carried so far as to create a character that looked like him, dressed like him, thought like him (implied), and acted like him... Mini Me. I realize the entire pretense behind all of that could be looked at as culturally insensitive, but it is an attempt to create ridiculousness to make us all laugh. I'm not condoning the approach, but it worked... I got a lot of laughs out of those movies. For those in his organization who disagreed? Elimination! . . . with extreme prejudice.

Why do I draw the comparison of a comedic movie to the hiring process? Because, let's face it, that is what many leaders do when they are interviewing for a position in their organization. I can honestly say I've fallen into that trap. The thought process of hiring like-minded people can be as damaging as putting too much chlorine into a pool. Too much of a good thing is generally going to lead to unintended consequences.

Too often, a leader or interviewer trying to fill a position or positions in their organization want to look for like-minded people. That is the best way to move their agenda forward with a limited amount of friction. It is also the best way to be thought of as the smartest person in the room. After all, if I hire a person who believes they are always right, and they think just like me, in their mind, I must always be right, too. The only problem with that theory is that, if it turns out you are wrong, there are no checks and balances to bring you

back to a right decision. There is no counterpoint to make you look at your approach in a slightly different manner. Creativity becomes very restricted. Your boardroom may look like this (all the time).

How did I get out of that trap? Experience! Through the years, I've learned that a good debate (sometimes looking more like an argument) is the healthiest thing that can happen to an organization. Having a counterpoint or differing thought tends to build on an original thought and not tear it down if those participating are open-minded enough to accept the counter-thought. Soon, I'll talk about some personalities that spark debate in the wrong ways, which can bring a negative condition to the organization. Don't mix the two up! But do keep an open mind to the concept of conflict being a good thing.

## IDENTIFYING THE POLLUTANTS . . . WHO/WHAT ARE THEY?

In this section, I'll identify a cast of characters I've created from people I've observed over the years in multiple business settings (companies large and small). The focus is on those personalities which I've witnessed having a less-than-favorable impact on the culture or outcomes of the business. For each one, there is a counter-personality (in parentheses) which can cause either equal or opposite impact within the organization. Any likeness these "fictional" characters bear to anyone living or dead is purely coincidental (my legal disclaimer). As you read this, you will likely be able to relate the description to someone in your current or past organization. At least I hope so. I would hate to think these characters exist only in the environments I have worked in. I sincerely hope that my identifying these personalities will be helpful in a couple of ways. For one, I hope seeing the definition of these traits might raise awareness of who is working in your organization and the potential influence they can have on it. Secondly, I hope you find some humor in the descriptions and have as much fun reading them as I've had creating them.

My Cast of Characters looks something like this:

> **The No It All**

> **The Bean Counter**

> **The Reporter**

> **The Attorney**

> **The Consultant**

> **The HR Hitter**

> **The Interrupter**

> **The Evaluator**

> **The Overbeliever**

Intrigued? Here they are, with their descriptions:

1. **"The No It All" ("The Yes Man"):** This is not a typo. There are, of course, know-it-alls in every organization. That description might also apply to the person I'm talking about here. I'm talking about those people in your organization who say "No" to everything. If it isn't their idea being discussed and/or they can't fully comprehend it, then the answer is *No*. Why is this personality so dangerous? For starters, they can quickly stifle creativity and turn virtually any situation into a negative experience. If this person is in a position of leadership and

actually has the authority to say *No* to proposals being brought forward, the environment may result in something absolutely toxic.

Another form of "No It All" can also be considered a "Hindsighter." You see them in almost every environment ... business, home, government, during a pandemic. They can particularly show up anywhere there is a need for a decision and no precedent to call on to make it. They could also be called "Hindsighters" because they are always watching out for their own hindquarters ... no decisions = no call for accountability. It is easier to make the statement "I would have ..." after you know more of the facts.

This is where you should apply the caution I brought up in the prior topic. Don't confuse the person who is trying to "play the devil's advocate" to spark some debate on the subject as the "No It All." When it is a person's normal response to say *No* without offering any logical reason why, "devil's advocate" is not the role they are trying to portray. In an environment where free thinking is encouraged and innovation is key to the success of the business, "The No It All" can have a profoundly negative impact. If you have identified those people in your organization and they cannot change their approach, it is best to remove them.

2. **"The Bean Counter" ("The Reckless Spender"):** "The Bean Counter" is a distant cousin of the "No It All." The reasoning behind their "No" answer is generally just a little different. First, let me say that I have no ill will toward accountants. "Bean Counter" is a societal description that has historically been applied to accountants. Some of my best friends are accountants. They have a very important role in every organization.

The advice they provide in order to support making business decisions is invaluable. They can certainly be at the table when business decisions are discussed in order to provide that advisement. Once they become a key part of the decision process, however, they have become "The Bean Counter," whether they are truly an accountant for the organization or someone who has taken on that role.

A "Bean Counter's" mindset is much different from that of an entrepreneur. If an investment doesn't fit into a Return on Investment (ROI) scenario, then "Why are we even talking about it?" Having an ROI discussion for larger expenditures is a great tool to add to the discussion. It should not be *the* tool for the decision. Once "The Bean Counter" has been immersed into the decision function with their ROI tool, don't expect to make too many solid "business" decisions. Could you imagine, in a highly evolving product market, if Research and Development (typically a very high expenditure in many companies falling into the "highly evolving" category) went through the same ROI discussion with "The Bean Counter" having the final say? I can ... there would be one less company in that competitive market. The same can be said about evaluating business tools or facilities or marketing. Once this evaluation process takes hold, and "The Bean Counter" is leading it, the results are likely to be less than favorable unless short-term benefits are the necessary focus, and long-term company health is secondary. If this personality, or, more importantly, this practice, is seen in your organization, it is best dealt with quickly before the short-term gain becomes a long-term pain.

3.  **"The Reporter" ("The Expert"):** This is probably misleading initially. You might think of

this personality being someone who spends their entire existence telling about others' missteps in order to further their careers. That may happen, but this is a slightly different personality.

I talked about "The Reporter" I am referring to a little bit in the previous Step. It is someone who listens to what is going on or has others who are responsible for informing them of what is going on. Once they have the information, they take it upon themselves to Report on it. Instead of giving the expert in the situation an opportunity to give the explanation and perhaps provide a deeper understanding for those who need to know, they grab the face time themselves and gain the perception of being the expert. It is very similar to the condition you see on television. There are personalities on the daily/nightly news who become the face of the news. How many people actually know the names of the field personnel who place themselves sometimes in dangerous circumstances and spend tireless hours assembling some of (if not all) the stories the personalities read on TV?

In some organizations, this person can become one of the top candidates to receive those unwarranted promotions or rewards because of the recognition they are constantly afforded. Eventually, this condition can and likely will catch up with itself, and "The Reporter" reaches a level where nobody can or will feed them their story. It is likely one that will take care of itself but not until the damage has been done. If this characteristic is observed, it is best to address it prior to the damages becoming a reality. An organization could end up with several managerial positions filled with underqualified people in them... then what?

4. **"The Attorney" ("The Defendant"):** Similar to my clarification comments with "The Bean Counter," I apologize to my friends and neighbors who are attorneys. My reference here is not necessarily aimed at attorneys per se. I'm referring more to those who attempt to act as an attorney with the intent of making sure no one gets offended, nobody can be seen as being called out, and nothing you do could ever be misconstrued. I would call those efforts an attempt at "Cautious Regression." It could be argued that stopping forward motion is not regression. I argue that, in a time and within most industries that are moving ever forward, if you are standing still, you are falling behind or regressing. The definition of status quo should change from being a static state of affairs to watching your competitors' backsides as they leave you in the dust.

You might ask how this character in your company ecosystem can cause harm. After all, they are trying to look out for the best interests of all involved, right? Like "The Bean Counter," this person is also a distant relative of the "No It All." The best and only way to call attention to themselves and stay relevant is to bring out why the organization shouldn't do something, despite the factual information at hand which would lead to a conclusion that they should. You might hear comments from them such as "I've done some research, and there is a small tribe of 27 natives in Eastern Asia by that name, and they might take offense to our use of their name in our product." I'm all for being sensitive to the feelings of others, but really?!

For this individual, it is best to look into their contributions outside of their "Legal Advice." If you find it is very little, it begs the question of "Why are they on the team?"

Sometimes critical action is required to expunge bad chemistry from your ecosystem.

5. **"The Consultant" ("The Owner"):** Now I'm going after consultants? No way! Sometimes, the use of a consultant is the best way to leverage someone's vast experience to help you navigate through conditions where internal employees have none. Sometimes it is the best option to retain the use of an expert inside the organization—you won't have to hire an outside expert at a high salary to navigate through a condition which has an end to it. If you hire them, what do you do with them once the condition is over? Unless they possess a broad knowledge and can continue to provide input across many business segments, they become an expert-in-waiting.

   I'm referring to the employees in your organization who dub themselves "thinkers." There are times when someone comes up with a great idea but is not qualified to bring it to fruition. That's OK! The employees I'm addressing here are those who make a living of it. These individuals may have come up with an idea and believe their part of the process is finished . . . it's someone else's job to figure out how to make it work. If pushed to be a part of implementation, they may say, "We have to *execute* the concept, too?" Unless there is experience to back up the idea that supports them creating a good path to make it happen, they really aren't adding anything that you couldn't create (in greater detail) by leading a good brainstorming exercise with those responsible for the current process. What do you do with someone who is trying to make a career of this activity? I think you know the drill by now. Assess whether they can change and become a more productive employee, or suggest they start their own consulting business.

6. **"The HR Hitter" ("The Promoter"):** My reference here is not related to someone in the organization who is always knocking it out of the park (**H**ome **R**uns). I'm talking about your **H**uman **R**esource mindset, which seems to spend time trying to find employees doing something wrong. Whether that is an actual Human Resource member or someone who has been self-appointed, it can create an environment of unease among your employees. For a person taking on that role, they would probably respond to that last statement with . . . "Good. We don't want our employees getting too comfortable about their jobs!" or "After all, we are all one slip-up from losing it."

Similar to my comment about the "The Attorney," this is their way of staying relevant and justifying their position. This is the same person who will create new rules for everyone because of an action perpetrated by one or a few. In a small business, this would be more likely addressed as a one-on-one conversation with the party who did something wrong. In a mid-sized or larger business, where an HR organization exists, there would be a higher likelihood that a new policy would be recommended and written. If many employees have repeated the transgression, there would be justification to create and publish a new regulation detailing what should and should not be done. I once heard it stated that the best company policy is that which is written on a single page with a single policy: "Do The Right Thing." I would add it could be stated better if it said: "Do The Right Thing for the Good of Everyone, Not Just You." As my wife and I remind each other all the time when we see people acting selfishly, "It's all about me!"

Could you imagine this type of action in your own family? If you had two driving teenagers, and one broke curfew with the car, would you tell *both* they couldn't use the car (new rule)? You might find that your college savings is suddenly more than enough because you might be down to an only child. The anger toward the rule-breaking teen from his or her sibling would come to a crescendo . . . beyond the sharing of personal items without permission. Of course, that wouldn't happen. You're a smarter parent than that. Be a smarter leader and/or HR person, and follow those same parental instincts. Address the issue with the problem employee, and don't create an issue with the employee who acted appropriately by instituting rules for everyone based on the actions of one.

One caution to everyone. The creation of new rules may help in some ways but produce challenges in others. Number one, there is the enforcement. Once it is a written rule, it must be enforced equitably . . . no exceptions. That's never created a challenge, has it? Number two, rules always go through interpretations. Court justices interpret laws in ways that, if their original creators could hear, they might turn over in their graves. Once that interpretation takes place, followed by an alternate interpretation, the rule has either been destroyed or requires a rule for interpreting the rule. Where does it all end?

One last anecdote to highlight the practice of interpretation. Let's use a simple statement to illustrate. "The sky is blue!" An optimist might interpret this by saying, "Yes, it is a beautiful day." An alarmist might interpret this by saying, "Yes, there is nothing standing in the way of something falling right on our heads." An ecologist might interpret this by saying, "Yes, and the reason it is sad (different 'blue' meaning) is because we are destroying it." This may be another silly example, but it hopefully helps enforce the point.

7. **"The Interrupter" ("The Listener"):** I'm sure probably everyone has dealt with this personality. You know, the person who won't let you . . . . Every time you try to . . . . You can never get a point . . . . They just won't let you finish! It is like being in a congressional hearing. The party doing the questioning is more interested in hearing themselves talk than listening to your responses. This is their way of expressing their importance. Their belief is that it shows their intellect but is quite the contrary . . . it reflects their ignorance! Either they don't want to take the time you will need to express your view, they believe they already know your view, or they really don't care about what you have to say.

Regardless of the reasoning behind the interruptions, this is one of the more damaging characters I've discussed. Not only is there damage done by not hearing the full story and gaining a full understanding of the topic being shared, but also the impact on the interrupted party is potentially beyond repair. The party interrupting has demonstrated to the interrupted party that they do not feel the person is worthy of even listening to. The interrupting party is thus walking away with a bad interpretation (his or hers) of the topic. They are likely going to transition into "The Reporter" role, explaining their interpretation having listened poorly, thus creating a credibility problem. Any guesses who will be to blame?

As a leader, one of the first and most important things you should do is *listen*. Listen attentively and with empathy. If you catch yourself being an interrupter ... *stop it immediately!* If you witness others being interrupters ... deal with them one-on-one (not through a new company policy). To go a little cliché on you, you were born with two ears and one mouth with the expectation you will listen twice as much as you speak. I have found over the years that you might be amazed by what you hear from your co-workers, employees, spouses, children, parents, *et al.* It could change your whole perspective on the person and/or on life in general.

8. **"The Evaluator" ("The Participator"):** Similar to "The Interrupter," this is another character in all sizes of business that can have a profound and damaging impact on progress, employee psyche, and general morale of the business ecosystem. By definition, this is the person in an organization who is in a position of authority and whose self-defined job description is to evaluate everything to a point of not making a decision. The goal is for everyone to develop materials to a point where they are auto-approving. I once learned that leadership is defined as the ability to collect 70% of the facts and have the confidence to make an informed, correct decision. Once 100% of the facts are known and the decision is evident, there really isn't a need for the leader anymore.

   That being said, there is a need for any idea being pitched to be as fact-filled *and* succinct as possible. The characteristic of "The Evaluator" personality begins to show through when the evaluation becomes more about the font size used to explain the fact and less about the facts themselves. Did you even try to understand the content? This type of evaluation has the same effect on the presenter as "The Interrupter." It leaves them with a feeling of disrespect. The presenter feels they have been disrespected by the evaluator, and the evaluator has certainly lost the respect of the presenter.

If you find there are people in the organization who take *only* this approach, do yourself a favor, and find someone more qualified for the job. Someone who is more interested in the content than the structure. Someone who is willing to make a decision based on the facts presented and not require return after return because they don't like how the story was constructed or the decision has not made itself evident. The innovators who are bringing these proposals to light are likely the same ones required to set the plan in motion. Once the hurdle of presentation preparation and approval is complete, it is said that about 5% of the work is done. If that 5% ends up being the worst part of the journey, those innovators may not be willing to set out on another.

9. **"The Overbeliever" ("The Overachiever"):** Not to be confused with "The Overachiever," this character can be likened to the armchair quarterback of the organization. Always lurking in the background and after seeing the results of actions taken, they are quick to assert their wisdom by telling how they would have done it differently . . . sounds similar to "The No It All." They are quick to insert their hindsight but not willing to step up when something big requires foresight or volunteers. This could be seen as a distant cousin to "The Consultant." The only difference is that at least "The Consultant" is providing the feedback up front. "The Overbeliever" will stay silent until their "afterthoughts" can be provided . . . then it's back into hiding. Boy, this is quite prevalent in Congress these days.

As I've stated with many of these characters, it is up to the leadership to verify the value of all of them. For every one that exists in the organization, someone is taking up the slack for their lack of contribution, and the negative influence created by them can be felt by all. Having any of these characters in the organization's "pool" means the pH levels can become more and more out of balance over time. I'll go a little deeper into the chemistry of an organization later, but, for now, you should be aware of how each of these characters have an impact. If the organization is a small one, immediate action is required, because it doesn't take much to throw the environment into chaos.

If it turns out that one or more of the characters defines your (the reader's) actions within the organization, you might want to rethink how you are affecting the ecosystem. Having the courage to go through a self-assessment and make the necessary changes can be very impactful. If you are the type of leader who can openly communicate with your employees, letting them know you are taking those steps can go a long way toward rebuilding trust and credibility between yourself and those employees. It can also lead to your employees taking the same action to ensure they contribute positively to enhance your actions.

## AVOIDING CONFLICT

The last discussion point in relation to impacting the balance of the personnel pool is conflict—not the existence of it, but the avoidance of it. For the purpose of this discussion, I'd like to start by defining what I believe conflict is. It can be defined as the disagreements that occur during the normal course of business. It can include but is not limited to conflict between employees, conflict between employees and leaders, conflicts between leaders, conflicts with policy, conflicts of interest, and any other event where somebody or something does not act in concert with each other.

Conflict that occurs in a business setting is far from unusual. Whether your organization consists of 5 employees or 5,000, there are bound to be disagreements that create conflict. The only way to keep a conflict from recurring or from becoming something much bigger is to address it head-on and fix the cause. The way to address conflict can be as simple as a discussion or as drastic as conducting organizational changes—or even termination when it has gone too far. The key is to get to it early so as not to let it reach the critical stage.

Don't get me wrong: there are very few people who actually *enjoy* conflict. A select few choose not to run from it. Even fewer have mastered the art of meeting conflict head-on and turning it into a positive for their organization. Those who have mastered conflict resolution should probably write their own "how to" book. It is certainly a good business tool to have.

> *"If we manage conflict constructively, we harness its energy for creativity and development." —Kenneth Kaye*

For this discussion, I'd like to focus heavily on the conflict created by differing ideas or opinions. One form of conflict avoidance, or so it is believed, is to hire like-minded thinkers. Previously, I discussed the practice of hiring a "Mini Me." One school of thought is, "If we all think alike, what is there to argue about?" Is that a good approach? I may have thought that way when I first entered into a leadership position. *"Build a team of employees just like me, and we can conquer the world!"* There is one inherent flaw with that line of thinking. There will be no diversity ... diversity of thought!

As I grew in my leadership roles, experience became a good teacher. Out of my 20s and into my 30s, I began to see that having differing ways of looking at situations might not be such a bad thing. That lesson was taught through older, wiser leaders I worked with.

They were embracing my thoughts even when they may not have completely aligned with theirs.

> *Wait—did they just stop arguing with me and start listening? Maybe I'm onto something here.*

Then, as I left my 30s and moved into my 40s and beyond, I was that older, wiser leader who started listening twice as much as I spoke (remember that reference?) and embraced the difference in thought. It became very apparent that a hybrid thought was much more impactful than a singleminded and potentially somewhat limited approach. The old adage "Two heads are better than one" is pretty profound.

Instead of taking the tack of hiring like-minded people, my approach was to look for diversity in thinking. Having employees with a background in manufacturing, finance, sales, and other disciplines is one way to build that diversity. It isn't always easy to see how someone thinks in an interview. That interviewing technique is a skill that has to grow over time as well. The process of mixing diverse people may not begin until you have had a chance to observe the members on your team for a while and then mix them together on different projects to watch the sparks fly. Don't worry—that isn't a bad thing. Sometimes those sparks lead to some good things, and, if you're lucky enough, they will touch off fireworks . . . in a good way!

I guess I'm maybe a little slow on the uptake. I should have been able to understand this process of controlling conflict when I was very young. Maybe you remember the old kids' toy, the Rock Tumbler, that consisted of a motorized base that turned a small drum full of rocks. It took a pile of jagged, raw-looking rocks and polished them into beautiful gemstones. All it took was a bunch of unpolished rocks (employees), some polishing compound (the leader), and the agitation process (conflict), and look what happened. I guess I was being a little hard on myself for not understanding the symbolism when I was nine or ten. If my memory serves me correctly, I made it through the entire process only once. Because the process of agitation was loud, my family didn't exactly appreciate the constant noise. Not to mention, I probably possessed the attention span of a gnat (no offense to gnats).

One key takeaway: the rocks referenced in the previous paragraph were not just any rocks. They were hand-selected because they were found to have the right traits for becoming polished gems. That hand-selection of the raw and unpolished employees has to begin with the interview process. However, the criteria for what you are looking for in that process likely will need to change. Instead of hiring people who "fit the mold," you will be looking for people who do not … that is a big mindset change. The result, once you've assembled that diverse group, might be a bit like the rock tumbler. It may create a lot of noise … learn to live with it. It may also create a lot of conflict … learn to channel it. And if it doesn't naturally create the conflict you would expect, you might need to become the catalyst to start it. If the noise starts to get on your nerves, remember it is just part of the process. After all, you are conducting somewhat of a chemistry experiment … and that is a discussion for a different Step.

ᛰ

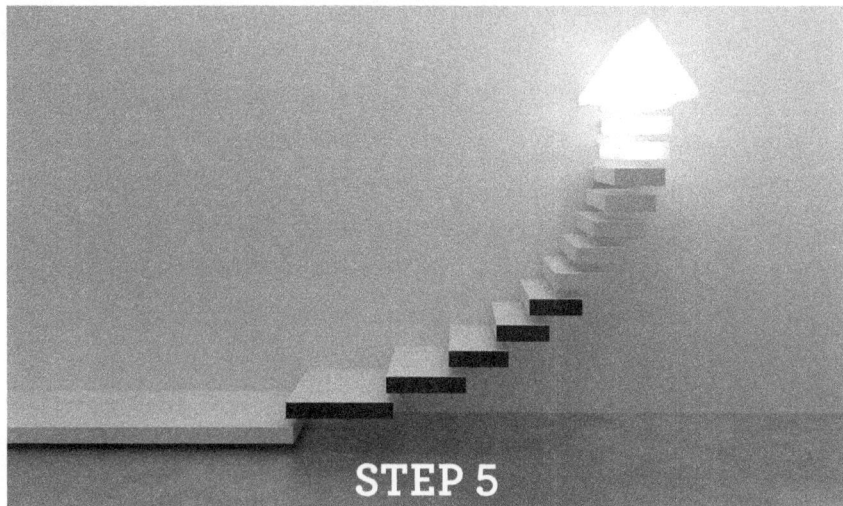

STEP 5

# Recognizing Chemistry ...
# Good and Bad

*In this Step:*
- Understanding employee differences
- Watching for "chemical imbalances" in your team
- How to create good "chemical reactions" within your team

**DIFFERENT IS DIFFERENT ...** *VIVE LA DIFFERENCE!*

As promised at the end of the previous Step, the next conversation will go into the chemistry of the workplace. It may be difficult to think about applying chemistry principles to the workplace. However, it is important to understand that there are dynamics in these groups that can be looked at from a chemically balanced perspective. Instead of there being a mix of elements, there are a mix of personalities, beliefs, and motivational drivers. I hope I can provide a better understanding of what I'm referring to with the following explanations and examples.

In virtually every business, there are discussions about diversity. Smaller companies are less inclined to have those discussions, but if you work in a business that employs a number of people, there are social pressures to create a diverse workplace. These are, of course, racial, ethnic, gender, and other similar pressures society drives into the workplace. That, of course, doesn't apply to the family. To take liberties with the old adage, "You can choose your friends, but you can't choose your family" . . . with the exception of adoption, of course. Similarly, you can choose your employees, but you can't choose your family . . . you're stuck with them. The interview of a prospective new employee is the driver for that selection process.

My use of the term "diversity" should not be construed as the types of diversity you hear about from social requirements and/or laws governing hiring practices. I'm talking about a diversity in the organization which is totally by choice and not "governed" by anyone. It is driven by the main person or people responsible for building the organization through the interview process. It could be argued that the diversity created by building an organization consisting of varying races, ethnicities, or other orientations would bring about a differing opinion. It could also be argued that making that statement could be construed as stereotyping the opinions of a race, ethnicity, or other orientation of individuals. No, I want to focus on the "diversity of thought." "What are you talking about?" you say? This is in direct reference to my comments in the last Step related to avoiding conflict. Hiring like-minded people is the easiest way to avoid conflict. Creating a diversity of thought directly brings conflict into the workplace. "Why would I want to do that?" Because it is the best way to spark creativity among the employees in a company and bring out ideas and resolution to problems. After all, isn't that what business is all about? Creating new ideas to help the business grow and prosper as well as solving problems within the organization or those experienced by your customers is a key tenet of any business. In my experience, the presence of "diversity of thought" has taken what started as a really *good* idea and transformed it into a *great* one.

> *"In business, when two people always agree, one of them is irrelevant."* —William Wrigley

I have already discussed an example about one of my childhood toys, the Rock Tumbler. Could you imagine how successful that toy would have been if it started with a bunch of smooth rocks (all the same) that were placed in the container to be tumbled for days and came out as smooth rocks with little to no change? My guess is there wouldn't have been too many sold. The function of that toy would have been completely different from that of the original. The tag line for that model would have to change to *"Annoy your parents and siblings by buying this really loud toy that has no apparent purpose."* Count me in! But because the process began with a variety of stones with differing edges and angles (ideas and opinions) and went through a highly abrasive process (the conflict brought about by bouncing those ideas and opinions off each other), they came out with a result that made the time and annoyances worthwhile (hybrid ideas which likely wouldn't have happened if everyone thought alike). Something beautiful happens! Of course, beauty is in the eye of the beholder. The beholder has to possess that open-minded viewpoint that conflict can be good.

The moral to this story if you haven't already arrived at your own conclusion? Embrace the conflict! Channel it so that it doesn't get out of hand and become chaotic or damaging to your team or its psyche. This is the role of a good leader. Knowing when to intervene with an anecdote or joke or calming words is a key to facilitating a positive result from the process. As this process gets repeated and everyone starts to understand that it is just that, a process, and sees the positive result of the collaboration, it will take less and less intervention. Guess what just happened? The rocks (employees) have just polished each other, and you aren't the only one who likes it. Now, if you throw in some reward for the behavior and results, they will like it even more and see a personal outcome, which will make them want to repeat it. Regardless of the reward, remember to celebrate the victory! It will help keep the positive nature of the process in the participants' minds.

> *"A good manager doesn't try to eliminate conflict; he tries to keep it from wasting the energies of his people. If you're the boss, and your people fight you openly when they think that you are wrong—that's healthy."* —Robert Townsend

If you find the facilitation, channeling, refereeing (whatever you choose to call it) becoming more and more difficult, there is one technique I've always found successful. Making sure all the participants keep one thing in mind is extremely important . . . *you are all in this for one common goal and one common good.* It is about creating positive results that benefit everyone involved in the process. Whether it is direct financial or process-improvement benefits for each of the employees involved, the benefit of a healthy organization (business, department, community, or family) is a positive outcome for everyone who participates with the right mindset. Let's talk about the mindset which doesn't match that description . . .

There are those in every environment who do not think for the greater good. Their concern is generally more focused on what is good for them. Of course, I'm referring to the Self-Centered or Narcissistic personality. I tried to find a statistical reference for how often or how likely you would be to have one or more of these people within your organization, but I really couldn't find anything to support it. I did find some interesting articles on the subject, though.

One such article, posted May 16, 2011, written by Jim Taylor, Ph.D., and found at www.psychologytoday.com, states that 30% of young people were classified as narcissistic. That statistic was derived from "a widely used psychological test" which also found that the "number has doubled in the last 30 years." In my personal experience, I do not find that I would qualify 3 out of 10 "young people" with whom I have had interaction in the business setting to be what I could classify as narcissistic or self-centered. That means we have done a good job of hiring the best young people who can work in a team environment; the percentage within some of our competitors must be quite a bit higher . . . if you believe the psychological test to be accurate.

Another interesting article I found to be helpful to explain how to spot those personalities is "How to Handle Annoying Behaviors of Self-Centered People." The article can be found at pairedlife. com and was written by Janis Leslie Evans. Here are a few of those behaviors she defines that should be watched for:

> ➤ Making trivial complaints about everything

> ➤ Throwing a physical or emotional tantrum or verbal rant

> ➤ Minimizing or ignoring the emotions of others

> ➤ Arriving late and making an entrance that says, "I'm here"

> ➤ Unapologetic about being wrong or hurtful (or even late)

> ➤ Dominating group conversation with interruptions or interjections

> ➤ Argumentative and arrogant, with a need to be right

> ➤ Overly critical of others

I pared down the original list she provided to reflect those characteristics I believe would most likely be observed in a business setting. You can get a pretty good feel for the type of personality that would be deemed self-centered from this list. After reading them, I had to stop and reflect on whether some might describe me. Situationally, yes . . . I hope not always. I find it interesting that nearly all these traits can be found on a persistent basis by nearly every Congressperson we see in the media.

If you find that these individuals exist in your organization and that they negatively influence or impact a positive outcome being achieved, all is not lost! There are two courses of action you can follow:

> ➤ Change it . . . by acting as the catalyst to "grind the rough edges off" the individuals you deem self-centered. This, of course, means through conversations as well as by setting the right examples and pointing out the wrong behaviors while being careful not to do so publicly, or by calling it out as a group behavior if it is limited to just a certain individual. This can take some time to accomplish but may prove to be very worthwhile.

> ➤ Eliminate it . . . if you find that the leopard can't change its spots—or at least recognize it has spots—this may be your only course of action to ensure that your team can function optimally. Elimination may mean removing the party or parties from the situation or from your organization altogether.

You might construe the last comments about changing behavior or eliminating as taking away some of the diversity of thought in the organization. I respond to that by saying: you can't sacrifice the good of the team for the creation of diversity. Forcing an organization to have the wrong people in it to satisfy diversity can be worse than having no diversity of thought at all. It can lead to no ideas being generated instead of limited ideas. The presence of this type of behavior can also lead to others being fearful to offer their ideas and limiting the creativity of the team.

## WATCH FOR CHEMICAL IMBALANCES

I'm going to preface this discussion of chemistry with: I'm not very knowledgeable about true chemistry. My last exposure was in high school, and I was an average chemistry student, at best. One measure of success could be that, at least, I didn't blow anything up! I can, however, state that my experience with *workplace chemistry* could probably be considered well above average. The art of creating the right chemistry in an organization is a much more pertinent skill to most of us. The principles are somewhat similar, though. Having the wrong mix of the same elements (personalities) in chemical compounds (organizations) can be damaging, dangerous, or, in some cases, deadly. If not properly managed, it can and will blow up in your face!

To put things into perspective, I'm going to use a true chemistry example of combining carbon and oxygen into different compounds. We all know the benefits of oxygen, right? For most living, walking entities on the planet Earth, it is one of the few things necessary to sustain life. It is right up there with pizza! **Carbon** and **oxygen** can be combined into several compounds that have differing effects, based on how much of each element exists in the compound.

The first example of mixing just one carbon atom and one oxygen atom creates carbon monoxide. We all know this to be a deadly flammable gas and is known as a "silent killer."

CARBON + OXYGEN = ☠

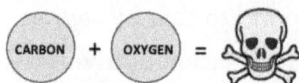

By changing up the formula and bringing in an extra carbon atom, it creates dicarbon monoxide. This is defined as a compound "so extremely reactive that it is not encountered in everyday life" by Wikipedia. By all definitions, it appears to be a rather insignificant or inconsequential compound, because, when it interacts with so many other things, it ceases to exist.

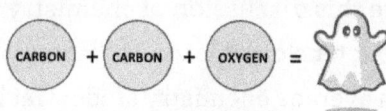

CARBON + CARBON + OXYGEN = 👻

By contrast, if you were to add a second oxygen atom to carbon monoxide, it would create carbon dioxide. With this mix of the same two elements, it produces a compound that will help sustain life in plants, which, in turn, use it up and expel oxygen. It is also a compound which identifies life itself, as we humans expel carbon dioxide and is a sign that we are still alive and breathing. But too much carbon dioxide can also be a bad thing. Everything in moderation.

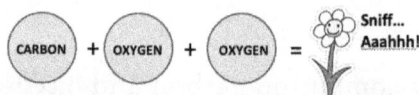

CARBON + OXYGEN + OXYGEN = 🌼 Sniff... Aaahhh!

We all know there are other gasses which humans expel, and, while it is all a part of chemistry, it has nothing to do with this discussion, and I refuse to go down that path just to elicit a laugh out of you.

So why are we talking Chemistry 101 in relation to business? I'm glad you asked. Just like combining the wrong mix of elements in a compound can have a dramatic impact on the outcome, so, too, can adding the wrong mix of personalities, attitudes, or emotions into a team. Here are some examples of how the right or wrong mix could play out in your environment:

1.  Mix two parts Strategic Thinker with one part Doer. What is created is a Distrategic Monodoer (spellcheck is having fun with that one). This is an inert human compound that only wants to sit and discuss what could be but never actually implements any ideas. Two of the parties in this unit dominate the actions and create inaction. The third party, who only wants to accomplish something, is overshadowed, and it becomes a wasteful team. Sound like any of your teams? There are times when this condition can be a good thing for an organization. When it is well known that some massive changes are coming that will affect the organization, but it is not the right time to take action, this can be the right compound for the conditions. The chemist in this instance needs to make sure the "Doer" is providing practical input into the "Strategic Thinker's" concepts. This way, when the time is right to implement, there is a pretty clear understanding of how the concepts *will* become reality. In a carpenter's environment, if this action is appropriate for the condition, this could be compared to measuring twice and cutting once.

2.  Mix one part Strategic Thinker with two parts Doer. This creates a Strategic Didoer. This would become an overactive, highly volatile compound that accomplishes a lot of things without much thought being put into it. Of course, the danger with this business compound is that many mistakes can be made that need to be corrected, assuming they *can* be corrected. The action of the chemist in this instance is to ensure the Strategic Thinker remains engaged in the implementation of strategies already developed. This would

be the logical team makeup to take action after the period described in the first example has passed, and it is time to implement everything created in that planning period. A carpenter might view this condition during normal times as measuring once and cutting (probably twice, since they may likely have to start again).

3. Mix one-part Strategic Thinker with one part Doer. The creation would be known as a Strategic Monodoer. Now you have a balance of two very different personalities that can cohabitate in an environment where equal parts Strategic Planning and Implementation exist. The relationship built between the equally forceful teams can teach each other and find the right balance to sustain themselves. This type of environment requires much less interaction by the "chemist." These conditions would exist during a more normal business cycle, where investment-dollar shortages do not delay implementation of strategic plans required to sustain the business, and continuous improvement exists in the organization. A carpenter might view this condition as measuring with two sets of eyes and cutting together. I can tell you through my own personal experience that this type of relationship between the right people or groups of people can be massively beneficial for an organization. Having had the pleasure of working with someone very complementary to myself over the years in these types of roles (sometimes switching the roles represented by the two descriptors), I would argue that the possibilities are endless.

The same examples can be demonstrated (with equally silly names) for Aggressive/Passive personalities as well as other traits. The real purpose for this illustration is to bring out the concept of finding the right balance within your team based on the conditions you face. Previously, I discussed doing a continuous assessment of the team dynamics and making sure they match your conditions. The same holds true in this discussion. There will be times where a heavy strategic presence is necessary and must be managed to ensure it doesn't become an overpowering force that slows or stops implementation. Likewise, there will be periods where implementation becomes a higher priority (such as when finances allow investing in the ideas which have been placed in the queue and/ or the timing is right due to the changes becoming reality). This is yet another illustration to show that there is no single answer and that the conditions must be analyzed to determine the path as well. The frequency of this analysis depends upon the type of business you are involved in and the current state of the business climate (highly volatile *vs.* relatively stable). You should establish a cadence for reassessment based on your characteristics.

Inside this organizational ecosystem, maintaining the correct balance is important for a number of reasons. If a condition develops of having too much of a singular element, the mood can shift from cooperation to commiseration. Simply put, like minds think alike. This is something to watch closely for. When that occurs, progress will tend to slow or stop, because everyone is evaluating the situation from the same perspective and viewing only the negative from that perspective. If the balance becomes too heavily skewed toward one area when the wrong conditions exist, the environment may become toxic or highly volatile. This is the time when leadership earns its place in the ecosystem and must correct the condition quickly. If the balance is managed well, the rewards are there for all involved!

## GOOD CHEMICAL REACTIONS

Again, there can be some amazing results from managing the chemistry within any organization. There are some requirements you should understand before you start, if you want to reach the desired results. First, it requires a good "chemist." I'm not talking about adding an educational requirement or practical background in the field of chemistry to any company BFOQs (Bona Fide Occupational Qualification). Being able to build, assess, manage, and mature a team should be a part of your employees' leadership skill sets. Not all leaders have this as part of their basic skill set, and I don't believe you will find much in the way of education to support development of this skill set. You may find a lot more business training, which promotes team building. Those may also cover how to build the team, with the assumption you already have diversity in your organization. From my experience, this type of ability is more of an acquired skill than taught. If you have someone in the organization who has acquired and demonstrated this as one of their leadership skills, I recommend they become the "teacher" within your organization to help grow the capability within other leaders. Creating an environment where the leader(s) can mentor others in the growth of their own skill set can spread the wealth faster.

Once you have established the ability to bring a diverse group together and harness the energy it creates, the next step in the process is to experiment. Unlike some laboratory experiments, there are really no formulas to follow. Referring back to my earlier comment that there is no single approach to creating the correct outcome, it takes a bit of experimentation to find it. The approach should be both cautious and continuous. As I stated earlier, the frequency of this process depends greatly on your own business characteristics and environment. Shifting conditions and/or changes in internal or external factors should provide the impetus for creating modifications to the chemical balance of the team. Sometimes you want an aggressive-leaning organization and other times a more-introspective group, depending on whether you are purposely intending to create a "Strategic Didoer" compound or a "Distrategic Monodoer" compound because the conditions call for it.

When you have attained some level of success, build on it! When you hit a home run with an experiment like this, you'll know it. There will be personal satisfaction, of course. Watching a plan you've created and attempted come together as designed and work to its fullest is a great feeling of personal accomplishment. Beyond that, there will be a positive chemical reaction. Not the kind you would get when truly mixing chemicals. There it can be as much *No news is good news,* like my personal assessment of my chemistry days: "It didn't blow up, so it must have worked." I'm talking about a reaction much like that of the "chemist" or leader. The team will share a feeling of accomplishment knowing they just went through a change that produced positive results. Do that a few times, and it will become contagious. You and the team will be better prepared to take on any and all challenges. Who knows? Team members witnessing the process may even develop their own chemistry skills. This can lead to intra-team adjustments being made without the leader's intervention and ultimately result in building the bench strength of the organization. Those individuals could become your future leaders.

ก

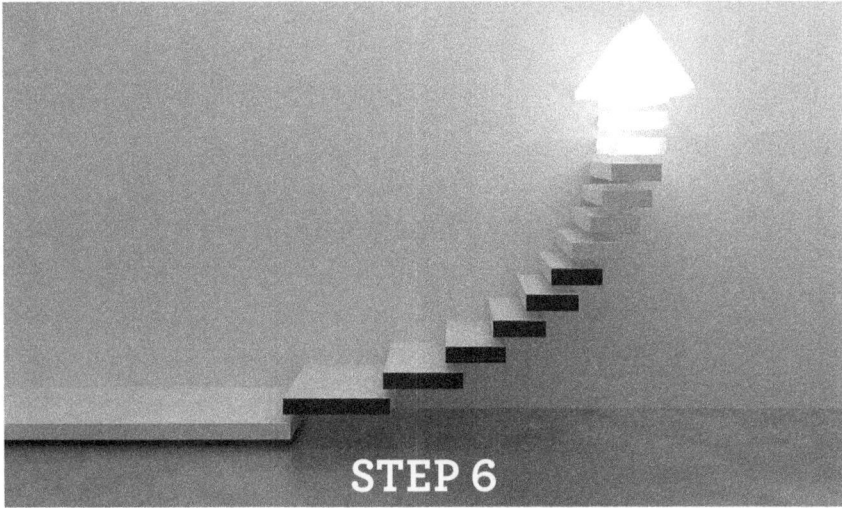

# Breaking Down the Business's Health Opportunities

*In this Step:*
- Understand the business conditions
- Evaluate what you found as potential opportunities
- Prepare for the journey toward improvement

## UNDERSTAND THE BUSINESS CONDITIONS

Before I get started with this section, let's do a little bit of a recap of the Steps already covered. It should help set the context for the next Steps. Sometimes you have to understand where you came from to know where you are going. That definitely holds true in this case. Since within the first Steps, we've covered who you are, what you are, where you are, and what drives you, understanding all of that will be a definite advantage to determine where you want to go and who you want to become. The reflection and opportunities are going to be different for nearly every company, and this will be a perfect foundation with which to get started. So far, it has gone something like this:

1.  In Step One, we discussed the overall health of your business. You know from having read that Step that it does not reflect whether you should offer flu shots to your employees. It is instead about whether you have a sustainably healthy bottom line and a positive, solid culture to keep it that way. We also delved into what drives your company. Whether it is "more of the same," the desire to improve or reinvent yourself, or simply driven, with no particular structure to it. We also asked the question of where most of your time is spent. Are you constantly fixing things that are broken, apologizing to your customers and employees, or in a state of constantly trying to catch up to your competitors? Lastly, we talked about where your company road map is from a development standpoint, a location standpoint, and the state of your business tools to support the direction. All of those factors and the answers to those questions make up the beginning of your organization's story.

2.  In Step Two, I talked a lot about a corporate culture. That included how it is formed, nurtured, and grown, as well as how it can be quietly dismantled without many of the parties even knowing it ... including you! An important part of the discussion in Step Two was spent on understanding how a good or bad corporate culture can have a significant impact on the most valuable asset of any company ... the people. If the culture is driven by the wrong things, it can easily become toxic. As I discussed, there is the occasional need to mold the culture to meet certain conditional changes while never losing the core. And lastly, we discussed the importance

of having deep cultural roots, knowing the warning signs indicating the organization is being negatively impacted, and recognizing when the conditions show up within your team. This is imperative for knowing when action is required. It should be one of the most immediate "call to arms" you will experience.

3.  In Step Three, I centered the discussion around how a culture can go through a complete unraveling ... and by whom and/ or what the chaos was caused. Since there are numerous things which can impact a company's culture, a combination of two or more can undo it even faster. Knowing the signs and being able to detect them was an important discussion again in Step Three. And lastly, we discussed how to fix things when you have identified the organization is straying from its foundation—*not*! I mean, we discussed how not to attempt to fix things when you have confirmed that the organization is straying from its foundation. Remember ... it isn't a program! It *is* about taking the right actions and setting the right examples. It is time to *do* and not *say*. The actions of the leaders speak louder than the slogans on the wall.

4.  In Step Four, I tried to bring out how employees, and, more importantly, the wrong employees in all levels can have a damaging effect on the organization. We talked about how the wrong employees can find their way into the wrong positions ... with a lot of help ... as well as the types of personalities and traits to watch out for. Lastly, I touched on how conflict (or lack of a properly managed conflict) can influence any environment. Please commit this to memory: *Harmony bad... Conflict good!* Not always, but if you want to get something big accomplished, add a little conflict.

5.  And . . . that brings us to Step Five, which you would have just read (unless you are skipping around looking for all the good stuff—hint, there might be gems hidden everywhere). In that Step, I highlighted a different view of the wrong people in the wrong positions or just in the organization, period. I've tried to give some insight acquired from my own personal experiences on how to watch for bad chemistry in the organization and how to create the right chemistry to accomplish things.

OK, you might be asking, *Why do a recap now?* Why not? My sarcastic side wants to say, "Because I'm writing this thing, and I can take whatever liberties I want, when I want." But that isn't the reason. The real reason is that, in Step Six, I want to help you utilize your copious notes from those first five Steps (sure, *now* I tell you to keep notes) to figure out where your individual situation contains opportunities to attack in the final Steps. As stated earlier in this recap, all organizations' conditions are different, and I'm trying to help you construct your organization's story. Understanding that you have a problem is the first step in fixing it, right?

Through those copious notes (or mentally stored references), you may have already identified areas where you have some opportunities to make a difference in your individual situation. To kickstart the process, let's review a few areas that can be looked at right away:

1.  **What state of organizational business planning are you in?**
    a.  **Maintaining or Sustaining:** You might be in this condition if you are fortunate enough to have already been through an improvement cycle or two. Now is the time to continue the process you have already started and compound success on top of success. Doubling down is a good thing to do in this situation.

b.  **Building or Growing:** This condition would exist if you have a business driver that requires your organization to expand on what it is already doing. The immediate need for growth cannot, however, keep you from assessing other opportunities to dive deeper into organizational improvements. It may slow the process as you focus resources on the growth, but it should not stop it.

c.  **Innovating or Changing:** You might find yourself in this situation if external changes are so great that you cannot sustain your business if you maintain your current business processes. This is one step shy of the next step of . . .

d.  **Reinvention or "The New You":** Not every organization or entity will reach this condition. Certain industries will experience this much more frequently and to a larger degree than others. If you find you are manufacturing rotary phones today, you may be way overdue in starting this and have already missed this opportunity. If you are making cellular phones, you might actually go through this process multiple times and with greater frequency, given the evolution that takes place in this industry.

2.  **Do you find your operations in an aligned state, or is it misaligned?**

a.  **We are aligned:** This means you have a business plan in place, and it has been adequately communicated to the members of the organization. It means all members know what they are to be doing and how their actions contribute to the overall success of the unit. Congratulations! You've got one thing going for you. Whether the business plan matches your business need could be another point of contention. If you have that adequately in place, double congratulations!

An additional measure of alignment would be if, culturally, you are in a position to support achievement, which leads to the next question (3, below) . . .

b. **We are misaligned:** If you have no business plan in place, or you have one, but nobody knows what it is or what their role is (hint), this will be one of your opportunities. If your business plan is in place, but it's dated and doesn't really have relevance to today's environment, you don't really have a business plan. After all, you don't break out the sunscreen when there is a 100% chance of rain, do you? Knowing where and how your misalignment exists will be the most important point in understanding where to focus your activities and how to identify the right conditions.

3. **How "clear" is your employee pool?**

a. If you discover you have the right people in the right spots . . . great; you won't have to spend much time on this one. But (here comes the big *but*) don't assume the assessment of your resources is over. Remember that, from prior Steps, I've said that there are situational conditions that take place through the normal course of business that might just "flip the script" on you. The best example I can apply to this is having the right leader for the right condition. If a company finds themselves in a state of being buried by their competitors, they are going to look to a leader who is known to be good at reviving or reinventing a company. You don't have to look farther than the auto industry during the past 40 to 50 years to find good examples of this. Charisma and no "BS" are probably going to be two of the key traits of this leader. The charisma will show through to the public while, internally, their strength has to come out to never take *No* for an answer and get things done. Conversely, if a company is leading in their respective industry, they may look for the type of leader who can be the right mixture of spokesperson, motivator, and innovator. In simple terms, that means they are going to be able to tell everyone just how great they are without sounding arrogant, fire up the troops who are already doing a great job to contribute even more, and make sure their organization continues to leave the competition in the dust by not becoming stagnant.

b.  If you find you have a lot of those less-than-helpful personalities defined in Step Four in your organization, you have plenty to document as opportunities. Depending on the personality being dealt with and the attitude they possess, the actions taken might be a longer process or one which is very quick. It is human nature to try to retain employees ... period. Sometimes, good intentions aimed at keeping employees happy and not afraid of what might happen to them if they make mistakes can lead to unintended consequences. I believe I have mentioned "unintended consequences" before and probably will again. That's important to remember, because sometimes bad things happen from what is believed to be good intentions. Not all unintended consequences are bad, either. That is why a well-thought-out plan is required.

The longer process is going to come about when you try to reform someone who does not positively influence the greater good of the team. Be careful not to "settle" for progress which gets them to "not as bad as they used to be." To create the highly motivated and fully functional team you desire, you really need everyone to be their best as it relates to the team. You may find, after some exhaustive efforts to bring an employee to their best, that it just doesn't work. This is a *good intention/bad result* situation. It is still worth the effort if the possibility of someone becoming more engaged and professionally fulfilled exists.

The shorter process comes from knowing the individual and having a clear understanding that they will never reform. That knowledge may come from previous attempts to bring them around or having a very clear understanding of their general attitude. Do not hesitate to hold them back from being their best in someone else's organization. If your initial assessment of the person's attitude and less-than-positive influence on the team is the right perception, you will probably find that the team will actually be relieved and fully support your decision.

## List Your Findings

OK, I'll start by saying "You're welcome"! If I hit on the right discussion points with the recap of the first 5 Steps, as well as "Understanding the Business Conditions," I may have just given you the "copious notes" to start with if you hadn't taken them before. Now we can start to understand where the opportunities for *your* company, project, or business team exist to begin to make improvements that everyone truly engaged in the process will appreciate.

If the previous content was revealing, or if I struck some of the right chords with the overview, you should start to list up all opportunities you have now identified. I would suggest you leave nothing out. Many opportunities are blatantly obvious, and you probably knew them before you even started this journey. Others may have become obvious as I shared some of the anecdotes and experiences that I have either witnessed myself or heard of from others. It is best to try to address them all if they stand out to you . . . but not all at once. This is where having a well-thought-out plan comes to fruition.

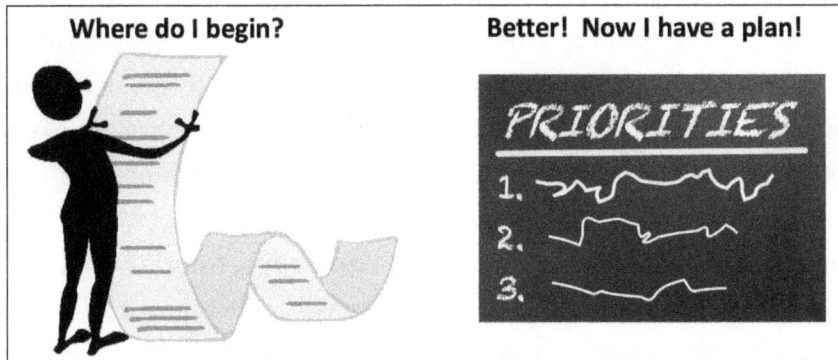

Now that you have your list of opportunities (an assumption on my part), it is time to dissect it into something manageable. As I stated, you can't attack everything at once. Not only will you become frustrated, but you might also just give up or forget some important points. There will be easy things to address simultaneously while taking on some of the hard ones. An example of that would be if you recognized there really hasn't been a good method to tell someone they did a good job. Now, I realize the first time you tell your son or daughter how much you appreciate something they've done, there is probably going to be a bit of skepticism. They may even ask your spouse if you have recently started taking some type of medication. Trust me, when it becomes a part of everyday life, the skepticism will disappear, and their appreciation for being recognized will stand out. Conversely, there will be actions which should be communicated prior to enacting. An example of this would be the initiation of a profit-sharing plan. You want your employees to know about that upfront so that they understand how their efforts will now be able to influence their own financial well-being by improving that portion of the organization. Making the recognition commensurate with the achievement level will inspire members of your organization to stretch themselves to achieve big things. Cupcakes to celebrate a victory go only so far to inspire.

Prioritizing opportunities defined to help in the achievement of long-term goals is a good way to ensure that recognizable success can be achieved. My earlier analogy of "Success begets success" rings true here. Once some of the activities are knocked off your priority list, and those engaged in the process see the results, they will become even more excited about moving the needle forward. Whether the prioritized opportunities outlined are driven by the number of resources available to work on them or are purely timeline-driven, it is best to make them challenging. Everyone in the organization should have the understanding that the strategy created is designed not only to improve the status of the organization but also the environment everyone works in. This is important to gaining the "buy-in" from everyone working on it. Be honest! Keep in mind that it is more important to bring about quality results than to meet a timeline. Here is another example of not "settling for good enough" just to maintain a schedule. This is especially true if you have been honest about setting aggressive targets.

I want to provide one caution . . . or maybe better put, one *suggestion*. The author of the opportunity list might just have some self-doubt about whether all of the opportunities have been identified. The self-doubt may be centered around whether all of the right opportunities have been captured. And what about the prioritization? Did you hit the right order to make the short-term improvements with the long-term goals in mind? My suggestion . . . send it through a sanity check! The best way to conduct a sanity check on something you have done is to give it to someone who thinks a lot like you, right? If you said "Yes," I'm not doing a very good job of making my points. Remember diversity of thought? Let someone who doesn't necessarily share the same views and opinions you have offer some feedback. If they have little to add, or you find that there isn't much disagreement, you nailed it! If they offer opposing viewpoints, it can only make your opportunity list better or more comprehensive. Either way, you could take away a positive if you entered the transaction with an open mind.

## PREPARE FOR A JOURNEY

Before I move on to the next Step, I want to make a few things very clear. Turning around an organization may not be so easy. Whether you are responsible for the success and operation of the organization, or if you're in a position to make a difference because you care about it or want it to succeed, the road may be paved with challenges. There is a potential that you are beginning a very long and difficult journey as you head down this road. It's OK. When Ferdinand Magellan set out to find a new route to reach the Spice Islands, do you think he believed it was going to be an easy journey? Of course not. He had two things going for him . . . someone who believed in him (King Charles I of Spain) and his own belief it would create a new way to run trade routes.

When Christopher Columbus discovered America, do you believe he set out thinking it was going to be a piece of cake? Of course not. Now the irony of it all: There are going to be unexpected discoveries as you undertake this. Columbus believed he had discovered a new trade route to India when he discovered America. Magellan set out to find India and did. Magellan also achieved something he didn't set out to do . . . accomplished the first circumnavigation of the globe. Although *he* never got to experience that feat, as he was killed in a battle in the Philippines, his expedition did. More unintended consequences!

First chemistry and now history . . . what's next, math? Just what is my point, you ask? My point is that the journey will likely not be an easy one. Go into the process with that mindset. If it turns out easier than you originally believed it was going to be, *great*! Prepare for the worst (mentally) and hope for the best. Another point of this brief history lesson is that you might find some unexpected things along the way. Keep your mind and your eyes open! Some may not be good things (like Magellan's death during the return trip and never experiencing one of the team's accomplishments), and some may be really positive (like Columbus' discovery of a new world which eventually became a pretty great place for all of us who reside here). The point is, don't be so focused on what you are looking for that you miss out on something amazing. Yes, I'm still referencing unintended consequences . . . both good and bad.

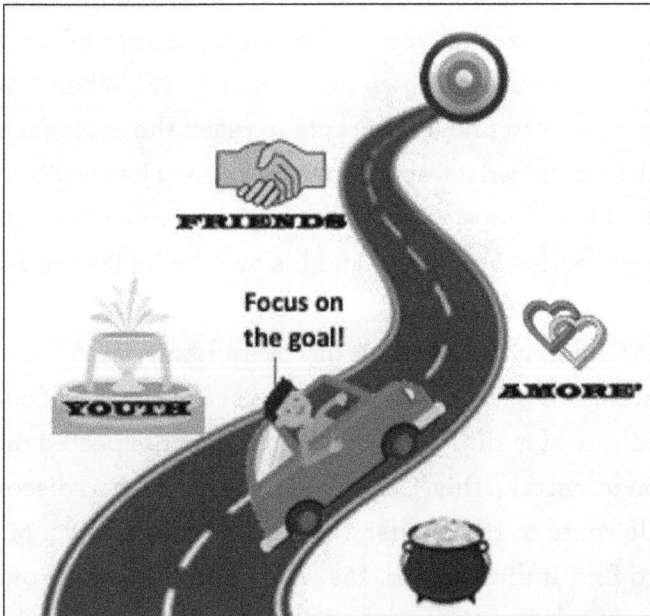

The final point of my short trip through history is that there are no true road maps (or ocean maps, for that matter) that contain someone's formula for completing the journey. As I've mentioned several times, every company's condition will be slightly different. This means that the approach you take will be crafted from your own two hands. Just as with Magellan and Columbus, there might be a general knowledge of where we're going, but they were also discovering along the way. That will be the situation encountered through this practice. Sometimes the party wielding the machete and blazing a new trail can come out with a few wounds. The key is to finish the process so that the wounds become badges of honor ... if only for yourself.

Please remember as you take on this endeavor, there *will be* both wins and losses along the way. If you want to reach the brass ring, you must be persistent. You can imagine that, during both Magellan's and Columbus' journeys, there were likely a number of wins and losses. Weather was likely a deterrent for both sailing the oceans. Battles along the way (which ultimately cost Magellan a journey-ending sacrifice). There may be discoveries during the journey never before seen by other travelers (or at least maybe not documented). The key is that, when you encounter these "losses," your persistence must come through. Navigate around them, plow through them, tunnel under them, or leap over them. Regardless of the way, show the team engaged with you that you are determined to finish, and your perseverance and persistence will not waver! ... And don't forget to savor the wins!

The last point I want to make before we start talking about how to potentially go about improving the conditions you've identified and achieving some of the opportunities documented is this:

There is strength in numbers! Don't think you can or must go it alone. Even if you can complete this journey by yourself, engaging others will help their growth in addition to providing diversity of thought.

Gaining the involvement of others on the team to be a part of the solution is crucial. Gaining the involvement of others on the team to be a part of the solution is crucial. *No, that is not a typo!* I just thought it bore repeating. While there will be activities the leader of any organization can initiate to move them toward achieving the ultimate goal, there is no better way to gain buy-in than to have others involved. Initiating your plan is much different from supporting the initiation of a plan which came from members of your team. Sure, it will take more debate to get to the final point, but will be worth it. The involvement of others will also provide that "sanity check" as well as expanded thought on how best to reach all of those golden opportunities. You will most likely find there are many who want to climb aboard for the journey.

OK . . . here we go. Are you ready to start the journey? I believe that, if you've reached this point in our discussion, your mind is right. *Let's do this!*

**STEP 7**

# Building the Right Team

*In this Step:*

- Understanding the power of building the right team
- Firing up the troops to do great things
- Detoxifying your team if it is needed
- Watching your team's "performers" rise to the top

## DON'T UNDERESTIMATE THE POWER OF BUILDING THE RIGHT TEAM

Now that we have assessed the individual conditions faced by the organization and established where there are opportunities to improve the environment within our area of responsibility, it is time to begin moving toward an improved state. As you have probably realized through the earlier Steps, I've placed a pretty high value on what I view as the most important asset you have . . . the employees within the organization. Their aptitudes are important. Their attitudes are paramount to the success of the organization. The former can be shaped through education, training, and experience. The latter *can* be a direct reflection of their leadership. Don't underestimate the power of having a team of properly motivated individuals.

There are three basic areas I want to cover. They can be summed up as follows:

> Motivation

> Balance

> Environment

*Motivation*

The most important first step in the process of ensuring every individual on your team is fully engaged, for the right reasons, and in the right direction, mostly belongs to the leader! I hope the following content will help explain why I believe the leader can and will reflect on the motivation of the team. Creating the right type of leadership in an organization will have a profound impact on how the team performs. It is said that people don't quit their jobs—they quit their bosses. Past Gallup Polls indicate that about 50% of those who left their job did so because of something their boss did or didn't do. How many of the exit interviews do you think reflect that fact? Do you think initiating change within leadership is not important? That 50% number is enough to get my attention. How about yours?

So, what does it mean to "sharpen the organization's leadership skills"? Does that mean everyone should take additional training on "How to Be a Leader"? Maybe! Does it mean you have to scrub the organization of all current managers and start all over? Maybe! Does it mean you should start acting with empathy when working with those you are responsible to lead, and go into every working relationship with the understanding of the following? Read my thoughts, and you be the judge . . .

Human nature drives us to want to belong to something. Of course, there are exceptions to everything, and there are always the "lone wolves" who, at least outwardly, reflect a desire to be left alone. Seeing that trait manifest itself in someone who previously tried to belong is a really good indication of something changing. A good leader will see that and take the time to understand what is taking place with that individual. It is the perfect time to exercise empathy.

During my own career, I have had leaders (not many) who took the time to take me aside and ask the simple question that sometimes can open up Pandora's Box . . . "Is everything all right?" The question wasn't asked because my work output or quality was suffering, so it wasn't because they were worried about their area. Could the change they recognized happening eventually lead to that? It certainly could in some but wasn't going to, in my case. They simply noticed I wasn't acting like my usual, interactive self. They were brave enough and cared enough about a motivated employee to risk becoming friend and counselor for even a few brief moments to see if there was anything they could do. That's empathy, my friend! And it didn't go unnoticed by me. Because of those leaders, my motivation and commitment never faltered. My commitment didn't waver for the company or the leader who represented them. I've tried to follow that lead, for certain. And sometimes it leads to a conversation you weren't prepared for, you were not qualified to support, and you really didn't have the available time to have. But you really shouldn't avoid it if you want to create a team of highly motivated individuals. That one person who views the commitment you make to them as it was intended because *you cared enough to ask and listen* may become the Firestarter within your organization.

> *"Leadership is not about being in charge; it is about taking care of people in your charge."* —Simon Sinek

Having the right group of people to lead any organization is paramount to its success. If those leaders are spending the proper amount of time being Cheerleader (Motivating), Delegator (Empowering), and Coach (Redirecting) based on what the conditions dictate, they can build the type of organization anyone could hope for. If the antithesis exists, and a leader becomes a micromanaging disciplinarian, you might want to start over. That means give them a chance to change. If that doesn't help the situation, give them a new opportunity (at your competitor's company). Harsh? Yes! Necessary? Probably!

### Balance

The second step toward "Building the Right Team" is to strike the right balance within your organization. That means you should be looking to build the diversity of thinking I've mentioned in past Steps. That means you should be looking to build some diversity in the backgrounds of the employees in your organization.

In a small organization, that can be as easy as adding one or two of the right people to your team. Simple, right? Well . . . not exactly. Remember that chemistry lesson: Adding too much of the wrong chemical to a formula can always be dangerous. The addition of too much diverse thought or background can change the dynamics more than you set out to. Finding the right personality to fit into that environment is almost as important as finding the right diversity of background. If you sharpen your selection skills, it will become easier to just know who will fit in, where, and in what capacity. I've found it is better to interview with the thought of interviewing a candidate for the company and not only for a specific position. A number of times, I have interviewed a candidate with one position in mind and hired them for another . . . with their consent, of course.

In a midsized to larger organization, it requires a bit more tweaking to get to the right formulation. That may mean you have to introduce a number of diverse individuals in order to get to a good balance of healthy debate or thought which is introduced from a totally different perspective. This also may mean you will have to . . . I hope you are sitting down for this one . . . give up one or more of your top-performing people to shift the dynamic in your team. One of the best—and hardest—things to do as a leader is to relocate someone from your team you have come to count on for so much. Many leaders may shy away from this type of resource management, because it will likely require more effort on their part . . . if only for a while. It may, however, be one of the best things for the total organization to relocate someone from your team. That individual can also help to establish the same type of balance in another part of the organization you are looking for in yours. That is a win-win for everyone. It is also a good way for others to see what a great job you have done developing those employees.

### Environment

The last part of "Building the Right Team" I want to discuss is the creation of the right environment. I'm not talking about adding ambient lighting and always keeping the room temperature at a perfect 72 degrees (although that does sound nice). I'm talking about creating an environment where an employee can derive both satisfaction and enjoyment out of coming to work every day. Mark Twain has been quoted as saying: "Find a job you enjoy doing, and you will never have to work a day in your life." This approach may help to influence the physical aspect, mental aspect, emotional aspect, and spiritual aspect of each and every employee. I'll give some examples of each:

> **Physical:** Providing something that motivates employees to come to work from the physical sense doesn't have to be large things. It can be a series of small things that lead to a large sense of showing the company values them. A large physical motivator might be putting a 5-Star steakhouse in the building cafeteria to provide lunches and offering it free of charge. Not a good idea, for many obvious reasons. Can we talk afternoon-nap time to start? But small things such as providing adjustable workstations, scheduling alternative food services on certain days, providing bottled-water quality dispensing stations, and occasional updates to the surroundings to keep things fresh can go a long way.

> **Mental:** The reference here is not to imply you bring a psychiatrist or psychologist on staff for your employees (although there are times that might be appropriate). My reference here is about providing things that can stimulate your employees beyond the mundane tasks of each day. By providing the opportunity to work on committees or take on projects both inside and potentially outside of their area of expertise, you can challenge someone to think differently and provide relief from the daily grind. If someone is struggling with their current workload, they may not be an immediate candidate. However, it may also be just what they need to motivate them to find ways to be more efficient, with the possibility of trying something new as that source of motivation. One word of caution here. Not everyone is wired quite the same. There are those who thrive within a mundane world. They may be very good at it and don't desire variety. Be sure you take that

into consideration before you assign something that creates a problem where one doesn't currently exist.

> **Emotional:** Appealing to the emotional aspect of each employee's life can come down to very simple things. Allowing someone to have pictures of their loved ones or pets on their desk can help to create a homey environment while they are away from home. Having a place where employees can commune with nature (a patio or a room in the office with plants and quiet) can help provide an escape, where they can get away from heavy thinking or a problem they are trying to tackle, for a short period of time. Providing a break area where everyone can engage in non-work-related discussions about family, friends, the weather, or the weekend can provide a social outlet where work can be placed miles away even if for only a short time. Providing these small gestures can bring about an emotional release for employees to recharge and face their challenges with the energy they need to succeed.

> **Spiritual:** Let me dig into a little bit of a controversial subject for a moment. I firmly believe an employee's spiritual nature can drive their beliefs and tenets. A company's approach toward "celebrating" one's beliefs while not considering the beliefs of others can have some unintended consequences. It is important for all organizations, no matter their size, to consider all employees' beliefs within the company before adopting a celebratory stance toward any one belief. This may mean it becomes an organization that "celebrates" no single group, but all employees themselves. If this is the case, then all members of the team should feel free to celebrate their beliefs outside of the work environment without feeling like

something they do not believe is continuously forced on them and they don't feel comfortable speaking out.

When it comes to celebrating socially motivated topics, it is better to remain neutral to ensure inclusion of everyone's belief. In a small working organization, it can be easier to both ask the question about what may create offense to someone's beliefs and celebrate some things. In a larger organization, with greater diversity, it is better to avoid them altogether. Regardless of the approach, in order to have everyone's full understanding, the stance taken through the organization's approach should be made known with the knowledge some will not abandon their beliefs and will choose to leave. It is bad optics and reputationally risky to show obvious prejudice by ignoring some groups and appearing to celebrate others.

If an environment can be created where employees feel they are a part of something and belong as well as feel valued, challenged, and empowered, the performance levels the team can reach will be surprising. If there is a feeling of enjoying what they do, and they can derive personal and professional satisfaction from coming to work each day, you will be amazed at the results. If you have built this type of environment, the next action is to sit back and watch the amazing things your organization will accomplish as you provide the right levels of cheering, delegating, and coaching.

## FIRING UP THE TROOPS

Let's focus on the motivation part for just a moment. Motivating the company's employees is not about holding a pep rally and bringing in dynamic speakers to get everyone fired up about doing their jobs and beating their rival competitors. That might work on teens, but as paid professionals, your employees are much more mature than that (myself being an exception, of course). Motivation of a company's employees is more about finding the things that drive them. The right motivators can inspire everyone to do what is necessary to achieve the company's goals, which, in turn, helps them attain their personal goals. Monetary incentives can certainly be a good motivator. That is especially true when company profit is linked to employee profit sharing. This is a great way for an employee to achieve a higher compensation, based on their personal effort. Not all jobs boast a mathematical equation of Effort = Pay (I told you I would slip some math in somewhere).

I once had a conversation with a young man who decided he was going into sales. I asked him if he was sure he really wanted to do that. The long hours, the constant rejection, the imposed sales goals (company- or self-) can be overwhelming. His response showed me he was wise beyond his years. He said, "I want to work a job where the level of effort I put in can directly influence the amount of personal gain I can take away." To me, that was the most anti-socialist response I could have imagined. When you think about it, he was exactly right. If you work in the type of position where your effort contributes only to the healthy bottom line of the company, you may attain less personally. If everyone doesn't contribute as much as you do in this environment but get the same reward, the condition of socialism has entered the picture. That is not America! Of course, job security is one payback. Continuous raises and promotions are another. There are also conditional factors that can influence just how much compensation you can achieve—even with the highest amount of effort expended if you are in sales. Needless to say, that individual has been pretty successful because of the attitude with which he approaches his positions. He knew his motivation!

That being said, one good motivator is to find a way to directly link the financial success of the company with the financial success of its employees. Effort = Pay! There are, of course, other motivators for employees. Some of those other motivators could be continued industry-best benefits (anyone starting or raising a family?), providing retirement planning and security, long-term job stability, and don't forget the personal satisfaction attained by achieving something great. As I've previously stated (multiple times, I think), don't forget to celebrate and acknowledge the victories. Finding the right motivators is important, and they will vary by person. If you can locate the right ones, your employees will be ready to take on just about anything.

So, about that celebration of accomplishments. One sure way to let everyone know how things are progressing is to provide visibility to the status and results. If you work in a small company, it can be something as simple as a wall chart to update progress on goal attainment. A simple sales-goal chart filled in by hand can become a good visual to let everyone know they are on track or need to work a little harder to get there. Using the tool to discuss the conditions deterring the organization from being on track and acknowledging it is not because of a lack of effort can re-energize the troops to push a little harder ... after all, they will want to beat the odds together. A simple Gantt Chart (see sample below) to track the progress of an important project can also be a good talking and rallying point to allow everyone to see how things are going. This can provide a task list, a timeline for completing them, and even an assignment for who owns each task.

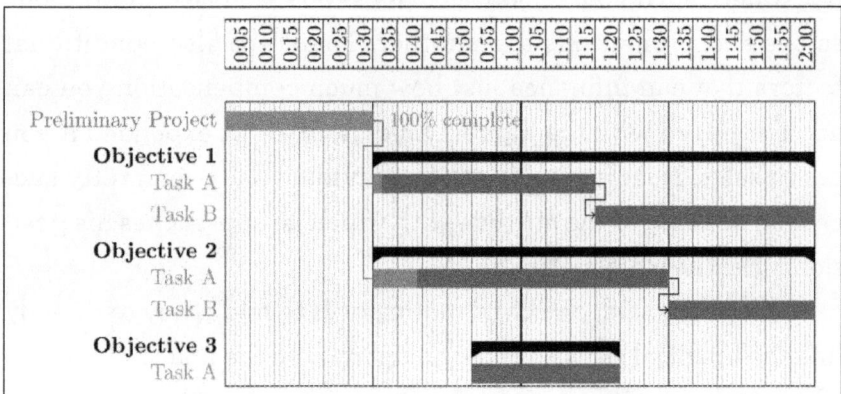

If your "organization" is a family, a simple status chart toward attaining something the whole family wants can be a great motivator. Maybe it's a boat. Maybe it's a lake house. Maybe it's a new TV. A simple "status" chart that reflects how close you are might lead to everyone working a little bit harder.

If you are a larger company, where you can't have intimate meetings with your entire staff or put up a simple hand-drawn status chart, it may be a little harder to keep the progress of the organization directly attributed to the employees' efforts visible. The concept can still be the same. The communication method will require some more creative thinking to allow everyone to see the status and hear about the details behind the details. Given our situation of being in a digital age, it won't take too much creativity to determine the best way for messaging. The concept is still the same.

The last component of the motivation of the people who can make the company successful is to help everyone see and feel the success. If the impact to the bottom line is to be shared between the company and employees, follow through on the promise. If the reward is just a "Way to go," then be sure you take the necessary steps to let everyone know they and their efforts are appreciated. Having a superior in the organization take the time to go to each area and give a personal "Thank you" can go a long way. Besides, it is always nice to see "the brass" when things are going right and not just when things are going wrong. Be creative, and let everyone involved in the achievement of shared goals see, hear, and feel that their efforts matter!

> *"If you care enough for a result, you will most certainly attain it."* —William James

## FIRING THE TROOPS ... THE TOUGH TASK OF DETOXIFICATION

This is the not-so-pleasant task of running any organization. Especially if you are like me and believe there is good in everyone. During my career, I have seen people placed in positions they were not "wired" for. Placing someone in a known chaotic and innovative world when they have thrived during their entire career in a stable and structured environment would be potentially setting them up for failure. That is not to say they are incapable of adapting, but I hope you see the potential before you make that move.

Likewise, promoting someone into a position because of their success in the role they've mastered can be a bit like assuming a fish can be put on land, and they will figure it out. The results will likely be devastating if you don't already recognize the ability to truly adapt. This comment is not intended to pigeonhole any profession, just to provide an example. Typically, accountants become accountants because they love working with numbers. God bless them! There are many people who will run away from a spreadsheet faster than Usain Bolt! Don't move them to an accounting role because you want to "help them grow." That is a bit of an extreme example, but this type of career movement still happens.

How does all that fit into the "detoxification" of an organization? As the leader, it is imperative to decide if performance or motivation issues are being caused because they became a "fish out of water" through the actions of the organization or an individual leader. Giving that person a second chance by matching their skills and desires to a position where they can make a positive contribution is as good a method to detoxify the organization as asking them to *seek other employment* (code phrase for firing them). If it is still determined they do not have the necessary means to contribute their fair share, then you would ask them to depart. As far as the impact on the remaining employees goes, most will recognize the effort to try to help the departed person become productive and will probably be happy they may no longer have to pick up the slack.

There is an unfortunate reality within many companies that employees do not get separated. In those environments, "problem" (or underperforming) employees just keep getting moved around within the organization. If you operate a small company, this may not happen as much because you can't afford it. It becomes very difficult to find enough people to delegate the workload to and not make a major impact on morale and productivity. Asking a person to depart is going to be very much welcomed by the performing employees, despite how much they like the person.

In a medium-sized to large company, it becomes easier to redistribute a single person's workload, and it not be felt as much. However, if it becomes two or three or four underperforming employees' workload, it will still be felt by the staff and can still create animosity in the workplace and impact morale.

My recommendation for the first act of detoxifying your workplace is this:

1. Remove underperforming or unmotivated employees from the position they are in. Discuss with them your intention to align their skills and desires with a position that may be a better fit. Relocate them into a role where their skill can make a positive contribution to the organization. If their skill is making coffee, I'm not suggesting you create a position for that. Now would be a time to suggest a career change to become a barista.

2. After observing the employee's performance in the new role, make a determination for the next steps. If they have found a new motivation and are providing an equitable contribution to the organization, congratulations. If the results are the

same, despite your best effort, it is time to say, "We tried" and ask them to find something that brings value to their life and someone else's organization.

You might ask, "Why go to all the bother of trying to relocate an underperforming employee into a new role to see if they can be 're-energized'?" After all, it would be easier to ask them to leave, right? The answer: because at some point, somebody saw something in the person that said they were a good fit for the organization. If they made a bad observation, I hope that person is no longer involved in the recruiting process. If they were right, then practice the empathy I've discussed, and ask the tough questions to understand what has changed.

After taking steps to either get people into the right positions where they are productive and happier and removing those who could not find either within the organization, it is time to build upon the team you have. This is the time to be very cautious to find the right "molecules" to add to the group dynamics. If the team currently has a chemical makeup of CO (carbon monoxide, deadly gas, silent killer), and you want to change it to $CO_2$ (carbon dioxide, good for plants, turns into oxygen), you know the type of person you are looking for. Maybe it seems kind of silly to relate this to a chemistry analogy, but I hope you get the point. You are looking for the right skill set as well as mindset to bring the balance within the organization you hope to achieve. If, again, there is a failure to bring the right makeup within the team this time and the toxification returns, it's all on you!

## CREAM RISING TO THE TOP

If the organization has become less toxic or non-toxic through the actions described in the first three sections of this Step, it is time to move on to the next level! On this level, the leader becomes extremely engaged with the employees from a much more positive perspective.

The first step to this level is to try to understand where the employee's "Careerpability" is. Their *what*? Of course, I made that up. Who knows? Maybe, someday, you will see that word being added to the *Merriam-Webster Dictionary* ... but probably not. My contrived word is intended to describe where along the path someone has progressed from a Career Capability standpoint. The graphic below may help you understand my thinking a little better. I've dubbed this graphic a "Success Box." Take a look at it, and I'll go into some further explanations.

"I Can't": Fully comfortable with a "job." Married to the mundane and loving It.

"I Shouldn't": Stays within area of education or title and is very comfortable there.

"I Might": Not sure of their own abilities but thinking about it ... On the edge. Really wants to try.

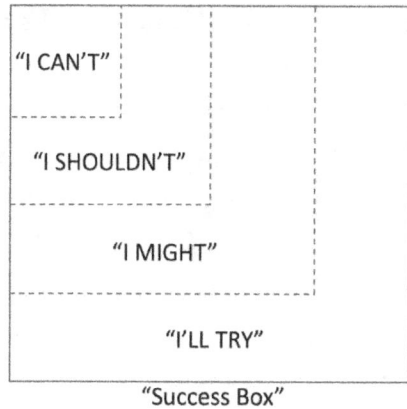

"Success Box"

"I'll Try": Confident enough to give anything a shot and, with the right amount of "grit," will make it work

The reason this graphic is so important to our discussion is that, from my personal experience and observations, the steps within this box represent what everyone goes through when they start a career. The amount of time it takes to progress through these steps depends on many factors. Let me put them in perspective:

1.  **Confidence:** Developing confidence over time is important to being able to feel like you can progress through these

steps. Being **overconfident** or having blind confidence can become a real detriment to moving at an appropriate pace. **Overconfidence** can lead someone to take on something they are not ready for, and a resulting failure can set them back in feeling comfortable to move on. That's not even considering the potential consequences of the failure.

2.  **Successes/Failures:** I've stated before that "Success Begets Success." Here is a new twist for you . . . "Failure Begets Success." Failure can be a great teacher. You learn from failure on an intellectual level just like you learn from success on an emotional level. If overconfidence gets in the way of learning from the failure and passing it off as bad timing (not my fault), then repeated failure is likely to happen. This is when confidence gets "rocked." Eventually, you might come to the conclusion, "I'm not cut out for this," give up, and stay in the "I Can't" mentality.

3.  **Conditions:** The conditions of an organization can be a large factor in the progression of a person through these stages. If opportunities do not exist to take risks and expand beyond current roles, confidence can never be built, and successes/failures can never be experienced. Ah, but there is an option . . . go somewhere else, where I can expand my career. This is where the Leader comes in, and I'll focus on just how they can aid in the development!

Every individual will move through these phases of "success" at their own pace and based on their own comfort level. The role of a good leader is to help speed the comfort level along by taking an employee completely out of their comfort level *often*. A skill the leader either has or needs to develop is to know when someone can be pushed along without either shattering their confidence or shutting them down. Everyone is different! I'm sure a group of psychiatrists could get together and provide a name for every stage a person is in. I am happy to relate my own condition to give an example of how to nurture someone through the phases of the "Success Box."

Personally, I am not an overly self-confident person. However, that condition is masked by the fact that I have very little fear of anything. Even though my personal characteristic would tend to keep me in the "I Can't" or "I Shouldn't" phases of progression, my ignorant lack of fear made me someone who always said, "I'll Try!" The descriptor for that type of personality would probably be . . . conflicted! I'm sure there are others just like me. Throughout my career, the leader's role has always been to figure out what was next for me to take on. Most of the time, the problem or opportunity presented itself in a clear way, and I would just do it. I actually built a pretty successful career out of it. That trait is very well defined in the following quote:

> *"I am always doing that which I cannot do, in order to learn how to do it."* —Doug Larson

For most other personality types, the leader has to take a much more active role in the employee's progression. Reading the employee becomes an art. The mouth may say "I Can't," but the eyes say, "Bring It On . . . I'll Try!" Accomplishing something small in this manner will start to build a person's confidence in their own ability. Even if, inside, there is a nervousness that moves them from telling themselves, "I Can't" to asking themselves, "Can I"? The confidence will take over and answer the question for them.

Where the "I Shouldn't" factor enters in is really important for the development of differing opinions. Sometimes you just need to have an outside perspective to bring about change. If you were trying to solve a software conundrum, and a group of program-mers with the educational background affiliated with programming came together to solve it, I'm sure you could get a result . . . and a lot of agreement among them. If you threw in someone with no programming background but could speak from the user perspec-tive, do you think the answer would be the same? My experience says, *"Absolutely not!"* That user might look at the situation and say, "This is a software problem. I shouldn't get involved in that." A good leader would push them out of their comfort zone and tell them their perspective is critical to solving the problem. If they agree, guess what? You just moved them into the "I Might" phase. They probably wouldn't have been selected to participate if there wasn't already some belief in their abilities to make a difference in the process. Their confidence just needed to be boosted a bit by knowing someone really believed in them.

In the prior example, just because they got someone to say "I Might" through their act of taking on the task for them, it doesn't mean that the leader's job is done. It may take several iterations of getting someone to migrate from "I Can't" or "I Shouldn't" into "I Might" before they are there permanently. As they recall the ner-vousness and fear of entering into a transaction like that, it may be human nature not to want to suffer through it again. . . . "Go pick on someone else for a change!" After all, can you imagine the intimidation factor of someone from operations sitting on a team with a group of programmers who speak a different language and at least initially wonder why a "layman" or "laywoman" is interfering with them solving a program problem? Not everyone is hardwired to do that. The leader has to see that in the person before making that connection.

In an ideal state, a leader would pull, coerce, entice . . . so many verbs you could use here . . . so let's go with *lead* every person in their organization into an "I'll Try" position. That is not likely to happen.

If the leader can bring every individual one level further, that would constitute success in my book. Besides, there is always opportunity for Round 2, as their employees become more comfortable with the leader and come to the realization, "They are not doing this because they like to watch me squirm." Employee development is one of the most important and rewarding functions of a leader. In too many environments, it is also where the least amount of effort is spent. Thinking about it from this perspective gives a different viewpoint of how to develop the employee . . . and the leader!

Let's assume (*I know, I know*) that, at this point you have developed everyone out of their comfort zones and, in fact, have created a group of individuals who consistently respond with "I'll Try." You might even have some who will tell you, "I Can." Regardless of how far along your staff is, now what do you do as a leader? Give them enough rope. No, not to hang themselves. To pull the rest of the organization along with them—enough to go and accomplish amazing things. This is the time to apply situational leadership based on scope of a task and level of experience. If there is a large task that has been assigned to a newer but very capable employee, you may establish more frequent verification stages and maybe even periodic consults to help build their confidence in the direction they are taking. Large or small tasks provided to someone who is accomplished and very knowledgeable might get fewer update points and less interaction. The real point here is to stay out of the way, don't be critical of the wrong things if they are inconsequential, and let them develop their own approaches and methods. You might actually learn something along the way as well. Keep your "I wouldn't have done it that way" comments to yourself if the results are being achieved . . . unless you bring them up to teach about alternative methods.

A key takeaway here is that everyone will reach a peak comfort level . . . some faster than others and some farther than others. Someone who achieves only an "I Shouldn't" level of success is not necessarily someone you don't want in your organization. If they have a good performance record and approach their job with a positive attitude, they have a place in your organization. They certainly would in mine! Even if they never leave the "I Can't" phase, they still may be a very valuable employee. As a leader, you should at least make the effort to grow them and assess just how far they can be pushed to grow. Those who move farther along can be viewed as "Cream Rising to the Top." Just remember, without the milk below, there is no top.

The last portion of the leader's role I'd like to bring light to is the role of helping an employee develop a career path. Having observed the differences among Baby Boomers, Gen X, Gen Y, and Gen Z (Millennials) through my career, I see one distinct difference. As the generations progressed, the next one seemed to try to map out their career paths better than the previous one. It now seems that career paths are so precise that there is an expected role and title for each block of career development. As a leader, it is important to share your own experiences, including the disappointments when you didn't make a title in your career and how it translated into other opportunities. If you found the same experience with your own career as I have, the best advice a leader can provide a next-generation employee is to *write your career path in pencil*. Making it too rigid will result in missing out on some potentially amazing opportunities that the party writing their own path may not have considered. Not allowing the career to often define its own path may lead to boxing yourself into a single discipline and missing out on finding a passion you never realized you had. And always remember to approach whatever you do with an infinite amount of determination.

☊

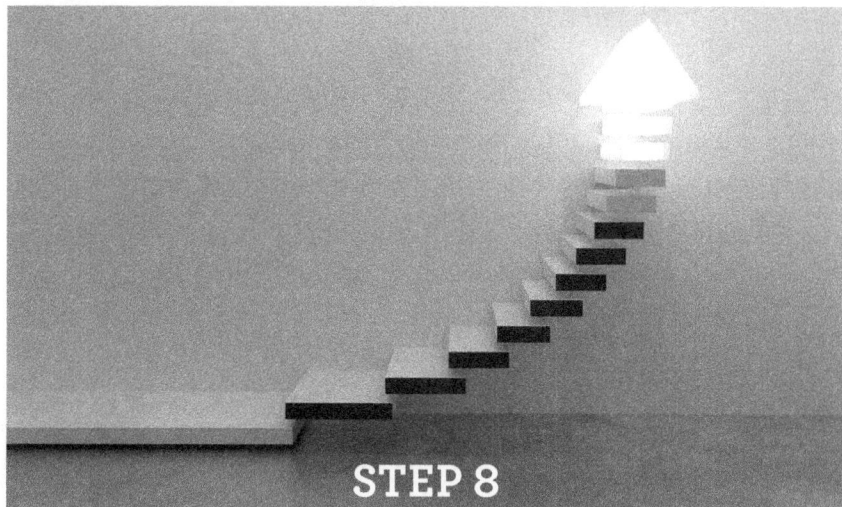

STEP 8

# Choosing "Grit" Over Knowledge

*In this Step:*
- Learning what "Grit" is
- Pros and cons of hiring "Grit" vs. Knowledge
- Making continuous improvement

## WHAT IS "GRIT"?

I want to begin this "Step" by saying it may be hard to comprehend the content as a true step toward transcending your business . . . I get it! However, if you can view it as a step toward selecting new employees, selecting an existing employee for an important task or placing an existing employee in an open position, you will soon see the importance.

If you have read and comprehend the Steps leading up to this one, you could stop right here and give it a go. Those steps were intended to help build the type of team you can be most successful with and identify the roles of leaders within your organization. I wouldn't recommend it. If you stop after the last topic, I believe you will miss out on one of the more helpful tips for creating the team of a lifetime. If you stop, you will never know, and you might miss out on building a dream team. Personally, I view this as the differentiator for what makes a well-prepared organization become successful. It is what makes someone not at all prepared for a particular position or task be more successful than those who are. It is G-R-I-T!

What is "Grit"? I have my own definition, but I want to leverage the experience of someone who has experienced differences in children who went beyond their capabilities to learn and succeed. This person also dedicated a period in her life to studying it. Angela Lee Duckworth has published her studies in a book titled *Grit: The Power of Passion and Perseverance*. She can also be found discussing her findings via her blog about the desire to learn how her students in New York City achieved success in her 7th-grade mathematics class while others struggled. You may surmise that is normal. Some students are naturally better than others, right? Here is the twist. After seeing some of her smartest students struggle while others succeeded, she decided to learn why. If her journey to become a psychologist in the pursuit of understanding why intelligence didn't always equate to success in her classroom doesn't define "Grit," I'm not sure what does. She had the passion to gain knowledge that might one day help others determine how to bring out these characteristics in future students . . . future employees . . . future citizens. Whether the pursuit of this knowledge was for her own curiosity or for use by others, it was a noble pursuit. Assessing a candidate's "Grit" during the interview process may not be thought of as an important recruitment criterion, but it should be. Finding the right questions to ask in order to bring out that characteristic in a 30-minute to 2-hour probe into a candidate's experience level and professional goals can be considered somewhat of an artform. If an HR organization decides to make this a part of their interviewing process, I'm quite certain they will look to find the right group of questions for bringing out the level of "Grit" a candidate possesses.

In Professor Duckworth's blog, she mentions that her study was conducted on several parallels. Looking at West Point Cadets, National Spelling Bee participants, teachers working in some of the toughest environments, and company sales employees, she wanted to find what made those who were successful, successful. That is where she identified the differentiator being "Grit." Professor Duckworth's definition of "Grit" was explained (and I have paraphrased) with four main components:

1. Possessing Passion and Perseverance to attain your long-term goals

2. Possessing Stamina to pursue those goals

3. Sticking with Your Future ... for years

4. Living Life Like a Marathon

Like Angela Duckworth, I have observed my fellow employees, bosses, business associates, friends, family, and acquaintances. It is interesting to see what made people successful beyond what they were "schooled in" or "trained in." Unlike her pursuits, I didn't know I was doing it and didn't document it (other than in my own mind). I didn't set out to create that understanding, but I wanted to gain it for the benefit of building my own teams. There are a few terms she defined which I must agree with wholeheartedly ... Passion, Stamina, and Living Life Like a Marathon. I would add to those definitions the mantra I've adopted in my own career, which is "Failure is never an option." If something is worth doing, the pursuit of it should be entered into with the attitude that you never want to fail. I would add that the perseverance comes from the knowledge that nothing shy of perfection is acceptable, but perfection will never be achieved because of constant change in expectations and conditions.

Once you learn to find and assign people with "Grit" to your business activities, you will be able to see the same things. In Professor Duckworth's blog, she mentions the question being asked of how to "teach Grit" to students. Her response was, "I don't know." I have the belief that everyone has some form of "Grit" in them. Finding the passion that stirs the embers inside is how a good leader, a parent, a spouse, or a friend draws it out. Here are a couple of simple examples of bringing an employee's "Grit" out. Placing someone with a creative mind who does not do well with numbers in an accounting role is a good way to suppress their passion. Moving someone who loves working with numbers into that accounting role from a marketing role that requires a great deal of creativity is a good way to bring their passion out. Let them get "Gritty"!

> *"Knowledge is power, but enthusiasm pulls the switch."*
> —Ivern Ball

Throughout my career as a leader, I have seen people who were pigeonholed into a position that was not a good match for their passion. Whether this was caused by a poor choice of studies matched with a misdirected perseverance mentality to see it through, or poor positioning by a leader who needed to fill a spot and someone was available, it is not going to be a winning combination. How many of us have seen a parent who enrolled their child into a sport that matched their *own* passion, but not that of the child? It will likely result in a bad fit. A good leader will see that situation as the perfect opportunity to re-light the fire. A poor leader will see it as that person not being a good employee. I've had a number of opportunities to place someone struggling in their current position into a new, challenging, and personally motivating role. The personal reward for the leader watching someone transform from being a "clock watcher" and totally uninspired at work to being excited about coming into work and sharing the results of their activities is amazing. Making a difference for the organization *and* for the employee is the role of a good leader. Making sure a child can pursue what they are passionate about (within reason) is the role of a good parent. As a leader in your organization or parent to your child, where do you fall?

Knowing when to tell an employee or child their passions don't align with their physical or personal capabilities without crushing their "Grit" is part of being a great "Coach." I am a firm believer in the idea that a motivated person can overcome nearly any obstacle to follow their passion. Sometimes it just isn't in the cards. For example, if my passion would have been to be a famous Triple Crown jockey, some good "coaching" to help me try to achieve that goal would not have mattered. Since I'm well north of both 6 feet tall and 200 pounds, it wouldn't be too fair to the poor horses. The coaching would have been better directed to steer me toward something else. I likely wouldn't have accomplished any of my goals.

You may find leaders who do not possess the ability to assess the assignments being made with their employees to properly place them. If you see they are either a) pigeonholing someone in a misaligned position that will sap any "Grit" they possess, making them more of a liability to the organization instead of an asset or b) inappropriately motivating employees by becoming overly critical of the staff and overshadowing their "Grit," take appropriate action now. Previously I spoke about "detoxifying" the labor pool. An important takeaway from the defined role of a leader is this . . . not all of them can lead. In the same consideration of "detoxifying" the labor pool, sometimes it becomes a requirement to detoxify the management ranks. If a "leader" of the organization characterizes the traits of "pigeonholing" or whose actions begin to stunt employees' "Grit" and growth, they are not a leader! If a leader fails to communicate the goals and objectives to their staff and penalizes them for not achieving them, they are not leading! It is now time to "detox" that level of the organization. Do it before you identify the wrong people as the problem and lose the trust of your employees. Do it before you see just how "Gritty" those mismanaged employees can be and apply their true passions to assist your competition at a very high cost.

My next statement is going to seem contradictory to an earlier comment I made . . . it is not. It was also an observation made by Professor Duckworth. Failure cannot define you. I realize I made the comment about my personal belief being that failure can never be an option. That is true as a principle. Failure in a segment of what you set out to accomplish can be a good teacher. Persistence to make sure you don't leave things as a mess can overcome a singular failure or even a series of failures, knowing that you will correct them and make the end product meet your original expectations as well as others'. *Ultimate* failure *is* and *should be* "never an option." The lessons taught by failures along the way can become the best experiences. When I receive accolades about my own expertise in my field by colleagues, peers and others, I'm always quick to point out it is because of all the scars I've accumulated over the years. Those can be physical scars, mental scars, or emotional scars, but all came with a lesson. Never fear failure to a point where you don't try, and you will never stop learning.

> *"An error doesn't become a mistake until you refuse to correct it."* —Orlando A. Battista

As an inquisitive child, it was not uncommon for me to question everyone's statements about different things. "The stove is hot" needed to be proven, in my view. How hot is it? Is it always hot—and for how long after it is turned off? It took only one time to touch a burner (I think at age three or four) after it had been turned off to learn a lesson and know I had no desire to question that again. Now, I can tell of my own experiences to my grandchildren so they can learn from it. If they choose to learn themselves (the hard way), I guess I can't say too much but only hope their experience is no more painful than mine with some discomfort for a couple of hours.

Similarly, throughout my work career, "Can't" has become a rallying point for me. Just because someone hasn't been able to do something doesn't mean their lack of success will translate to failure by someone with the right amount of passion and perseverance ("Grit") to see it through. How satisfying it is for someone who pulls off something that was believed to be impossible. How regretful it is for those who tried and quit. Even more regretful for those who wanted to, but never tried, and have missed out on knowing if they could have been successful or knowing the feeling of celebrating the success. It is my belief that the only thing that should be regretted is that which was never tried. Successes should always be expected when you set out to accomplish something. Surprise successes (things you tried but weren't sure about) can be seen as true bonuses in life. Failures born from trying (whether difficult or believed impossible) are life's professors in the School of Hard Knocks! No teacher or professor in a classroom can measure up to those lessons learned.

> *"It's kind of fun to do the impossible."* —Walt Disney

So, you see, failure can be a wonderful (and sometimes painful) teacher. Learning to know what to do from the successes, as well as what not to do from the failures, are equally important in life. But the bottom line is: You can't learn if you don't try! You also can't succeed!

There is a lot to be learned from a formal education, but it is just the basis for learning. From my perspective, experience is the best teacher. Taking away a lesson from both success and failures better prepares a person to repeat the success or modify the behavior to turn the failure into success the next time. Being open to continuously learning in every aspect of life is really all it takes to get there. Remembering there is more that you don't know than what you do know will unlock the greatest potential!

Where does perseverance come from? If you wish to find a good example, look no further than an elite athlete in their sport. They are the epitome of failure not defining them. An athlete who can, within a single competition, remember what caused a particular failure, correct it but forget that it happened, and reapply themselves toward the end goal will be more successful than those who dwell on a single failure and lose sight (even if for only a short time) of that goal. In mathematical terms (that I promised to blend in), this formula would look something like S = F x F. Translated, it would read Success = Failure x "Forget About It." Letting it go is difficult sometimes, but, in the end, you will be better off. Learning a lesson from an athlete whose talents are well beyond your own can be quite humbling. Seeing how bad you are at a sport they excel in goes beyond the physical. If we can set the humility aside and learn the single lesson of the "Let it go" part of the mental aspect of their game, it can teach us a lot. Think about this the next time you watch any sport to see who does it well and who does not. This is where their "Never give up" attitude comes from. Those who forget the "Forget About It" part will be smashing bats or racquets or throwing things they are not supposed to be . . . and then again, sometimes that is the release of frustration that helps the process along. Been there!

## LET'S DEBATE: "GRIT" OR KNOWLEDGE . . . WHICH IS BEST?

Let's start a little debate, shall we? Unfortunately, we can't have a back-and-forth through this medium, so I guess you get the last word . . . but I don't have to listen to it. Not ideal, but I hope it is still fun. Throughout this content, I've tried to blend experiences and opinions, and I hope you will find a good mix of both during the discussion of the importance of "Grit" and knowledge.

I'll start with the condition where "Grit" exists, but knowledge does not. More and more, I am seeing individuals' passion about a subject without true knowledge of the subject matter. This can happen when a political faction states their opinion about a subject, and the loyal followers follow, not knowing from their own firsthand knowledge or experience if it is right. This has never been more prevalent than during the COVID-19 Pandemic. Someone else's opinion (not knowledge) combining with an individual's passion being applied blindly can be a very dangerous thing. Some dangerous unintended consequences can result from an individual passionately acting on what they *think* versus what they *know*.

Here's an example (with my upfront apology for the violent nature): You might be a person who is passionate about aiding those who cannot defend themselves. Let's suppose you walk into a room and find a larger person physically restraining a smaller individual on the ground rather roughly. Lying nearby is a third individual who has obviously been badly beaten. Given your human nature, we will assume your first reaction is *not* to pull out your cell phone and video. You passionately step in and blindside the larger person to keep the smaller person from suffering the same fate as the third individual lying on the floor. You just reacted to what you *think* you know, based on seeing the situation in front of you. What you don't know is that the larger individual shares your passion for helping those unable to help themselves. They walked in on the person they were restraining badly beating the third party and stopped them. By freeing the smaller man who was restrained, you allowed an assailant to get away and harmed a Good Samaritan while trying to be a Good Samaritan yourself. Applying your passion to what you *think* versus what you *know* can be a big difference maker.

Professor Duckworth stated in her blog that she responded to a question from a teacher of "How do I teach "Grit" to my students' with: "I don't know." I agree with that statement. My belief is you cannot teach "Grit." As I stated earlier, I believe it is in everyone. The level it is present will vary. What brings it out of an individual will also vary. I also believe what is required as a leader is to find what each individual is passionate about or truly enjoys and draw the "Grit" out of them. It is like igniting a flame inside each person and then providing the fuel to keep it burning. The fuel at this point can be as simple as a congratulatory remark or giving them more responsibility in their role. This is a good example of why it is important to detect an interviewee's "Grit" level during the interview process. Not only should you find whether an interviewee has "Grit" but also if it is aligned with what you do, or, more importantly, what tasks you have in mind for them.

How do you learn an interviewee's "Grit" level during an interview? The best method I have learned is to find what a person is passionate about. It may present itself during the interview process, or you might just have to ask. Even if their passion is not necessarily related to the job you are interviewing them for, you can learn quite a bit about just how much "Grit" is present in them. Bring the conversation around to the position, and see if the excitement carriers over. Once you wind an interviewee up, it will be difficult to curb the enthusiasm. If it carries through to the position specifics, you may have a good foundation for success.

Conversely, the condition can occur where knowledge about something exists, but no passion or "Grit" does. How does that happen? Simple! If you are exposed to something and learn about it but don't really care about it, the situation exists. During high school, you are required to take specific courses to "round out" your education. Were you passionate about all of those subjects? I know my answer to that question . . . "yawn. . . ." In college, the same logic is applied, and students are pushed to take electives. Can you honestly state you didn't take an "easy A" class the subject matter about which you couldn't care less? How passionate were you about pursuing that as a career? There are, of course, exceptions to that rule where you might have been exposed to something you wouldn't have otherwise taken and wouldn't have known you had a passion for, but I would surmise it is just that . . . the exception.

The condition can also exist where you find yourself in a career choice that doesn't really stir your passion or perseverance. There will be many who ask, *How do you possibly get into that situation?* If you are following in the family tradition of working for the family business, that can happen. The American farm industry is a good example of that. It is well documented that children are not very enthusiastic about carrying on the family farm. Larger "corporate" farming operations are becoming the norm, and the small family farm is becoming scarcer. Maybe you have followed a friend's influence into their career choice based on their passion for it. The allure sounded really good at the time, and job opportunities were everywhere, but now you are finding that wasn't the best choice for you. Now you have the knowledge and the skills but no "Grit" to apply to it. You could be fortunate enough to have that knowledge or skill carry into other career opportunities about which you are more passionate.

It is possible to find yourself in those types of circumstances. You might even be what I would call "miserably successful." In that situation, the business is sustaining you, and you are not applying yourself to successfully sustain the business. It is likely just a matter of time before you decide or unknowingly find yourself in a condition where failure *is* an option. The business may quit you, or you may quit the business. If you are an individual who eats challenges and spits "Grit," you may also someday acquire the same passion for the business your family before you had, but for different reasons. The challenge of keeping the family business together for future generations may also be a major motivator and what you apply your "Grit" toward. Remember to always consider that "penciled career path" I mentioned before, in the event you find the current one unsustainable.

The condition can also exist where "Knowledge" meets "Grit." If you are personally in this situation, you are likely going to be motivated out of your mind to do something. Your chosen career path (or the one which chose you) matches the education or experience you have gained. Good for you! If you find you have employees in this situation, you are in a position of accomplishing more than you could imagine. Don't mess it up! Leaders (I use that term loosely in this context) who make a mess of this condition are likely to be very unsure of their own ability, don't want to be outshone, or are just plain incompetent. Over-managing these types of individuals or applying too many rules and restrictions on their activities are ways to erode their "Grit." These are the types of "leaders" who need to be exorcised from the organization. A good leader, on the other hand, will find a way to "feed the beast"! Give the right amount of motivation and guidance just to keep these individuals moving at the speed of which they are capable. Oh, and don't be overly critical if they make a couple of mistakes along the way (remember the lessons that come from it) or outshine you from time to time.

There is also, in my belief, another condition where "Grit" is present. An individual can be passionate about multiple things. The subject which motivates them can be something either in which they are already knowledgeable or have a strong desire to become knowledgeable in. That passion or motivation can come in numerous forms.

For example, if a loved one suffers from a debilitating or even life-threatening illness, you might generate a strong desire to learn more about it *and* become very passionate about influencing the outcomes for future generations. The passion may carry an individual to professionally educate to become a part of research and development to find a cure for the condition their loved one has suffered with. Equally as important, they may want to learn how they can contribute time and resources to influence that research as a volunteer.

Professionally, an individual may witness something impacting their organization which doesn't seem to be getting addressed. It could be an influence which is impacting their own monetary reward and the incomes of those around them. It could be something which is creating higher stress or hindering their ability to achieve successful performance of their job. Regardless, development of a passion to correct the condition while having no knowledge of the subject can drive them to learn and make a difference.

Here is where I interject my opinion (if you haven't seen evidence to this point) about the subject of "Grit" and where and how it exists. My belief is that "Grit" can exist on multiple levels. It can be a personal trait which is just dying to get out and be applied toward something that becomes an interest. It can be a situational attribute that is stirred by one of the events I've mentioned. Regardless of the condition that creates "Grit" in an individual, it is up to the leader to apply it properly. If "Grit" is a personal trait, a good leader will stoke the flame. By listening to what becomes of interest to their employees and continually teaching or facilitating their education, an employee can find their way toward making a big difference for the organization. If "Grit" is a situational condition, it is up to the leader to recognize the best role for the individual and find a way to position them in that role to be successful.

With all my discussion on the topic and focus on "Grit" as a business tool just waiting to be applied to the right situation, you can probably surmise that I would choose "Grit" over "Knowledge" if I can't find the right mix of both. If that's what you think, you would be correct! As I've said, you can build knowledge . . . you can't teach "Grit"!

## MOVING THE NEEDLE

What is meant by the term "moving the needle"? I'm referring to constantly propelling your organization toward being the best it can be. It means beating your competition. It means beating your last recorded sales result. It means beating your last recorded profit result. It means achieving your best result in a personal endeavor. You get the picture. If, as an organization, you are not advancing, you are standing still. Standing still makes you a stationary target . . . not only for your competition, but for complacency and apathy to enter your organization.

How do you stop that from happening? Create an environment of continuous improvement! This should be the goal of every leader. Keeping to the adage of "If it ain't broke, don't fix it" is dangerous for any organization. My personal viewpoint is that the best way to keep an organization from becoming stagnant, and a stationary target, is to adopt the philosophy "If it ain't broke, improve it!" Expanding on something that is working is a much better approach than letting it operate without any attention until it breaks. Choose nurturing over using. Choose maintaining your business tools over maintaining the status quo.

The best approach to establishing this type of environment within your organization is to find employees who possess "Grit" and "Knowledge" and who want to support this type of activity and belief. If they don't exist inside your own organization, you may have to go find them. If they do, it is time to be the leader I've been referring to. If you have employees who have the passion to help but not the knowledge, teach them what they need to know, or help them obtain the knowledge. If you have employees who possess both "Grit" and "Knowledge," position them in the proper roles to make a difference and give them the guidance and support they need to succeed on your behalf. These same individuals can also become great teachers to provide the knowledge for those who have the passion and willingness to learn.

Now here is a revelation for anyone who has followed along thus far. As I revealed, innovation should be a part of a company's culture. There may have been a tendency to view this only as something a large company can do. That would be a wrong assumption. There is a reason for not calling out activities that apply to specific sizes of organizations. These activities apply to all organizations. The approaches just might be a little different.

If you are a part of a small operation (let's say fewer than 100 employees), creating a culture of innovation can be even more impactful than that of a medium-sized to large organization. How, you say? It is simple physics (not again!). Diluting a small pool of water is much simpler than diluting the ocean. It requires much less effort to make an immediate and profound impact. The pool of employees from which to find an employee who possesses both "Grit" and "Knowledge" is smaller, but the task is certainly not impossible. The opportunity to create an impact is much greater, and the probability that the enthusiasm will wear off on others is more likely. The leader's role in this environment is no different from any other organization . . . nurture, support, and reward where the situation calls for it.

If you are a part of a medium-sized or larger organization, the pool available for finding potential innovation leaders who possess "Grit" and "Knowledge" will be larger . . . the good news! Unfortunately, the likelihood of the employees' roles to be more specialized and segmented is greater, and they may not possess the breadth of knowledge someone in a smaller organization might. That is where the approach must be different and tailored to the situation.

An organization in which there isn't a qualified individual with whom to create an environment of innovation across all disciplines, creating a team with members from each discipline represented is a good alternative. Those qualified individuals who possess both "Grit" and "Knowledge" to apply within their business discipline can feed off each other's passion as well as learn from each other and expand their knowledge of the total business (create the desired breadth of knowledge). In a multi-location organization, an innovation team can become a corporation's "change agency," capable of providing insight, consultation, and improvements to multiple sites and departments while harmonizing the needed actions of all the departments.

An example where cross-functional innovation is required within only a couple of disciplines, instead of at the corporate level, might be where a condition exists between manufacturing and accounting where capturing cost and reporting needs to be improved. In a larger organization, finding an individual capable *and* knowledgeable—let alone passionate about both areas—would be very unlikely. Finding the right people in each discipline to work together to create improvement to existing processes would be a better approach. Like the analogy, used earlier, of putting these two "Gritty" people together to work on a solution would be like placing them in a rock tumbler together with the hope of achieving a polished result of growth in knowledge of each other's discipline and a solution to your problem.

There is a lot of talk and action taken in Corporate America to create "Diversity" in the organization. Diversity is defined as a good blend of races, ethnicities, genders, etc. As stated before, there is a diversity to be gained through many of these group innovation activities which will transcend those descriptors by building on each involved party's strengths to overcome weaknesses through "diversity of thought." Placing the right person in the right role, at the right time, is a brilliant way to bring out the results you want. Letting the "Rocks" tumble against each other gets the polished outcome any good leader would hope to achieve.

In another sports analogy, the use of a Designated Hitter within the American League of Major League Baseball is such an example. This could be a good representation of a larger corporation where the task within each business segment is large enough that specialization is required. In the Designated Hitter example, the American League decided to let the hitters work on what they do best and practice hitting as well as let the pitchers focus on what they do best and hone primarily their pitching skills. They both can be passionate about their trade (hitting or pitching) within the strategy of the game of baseball, and the team can be successful.

Reading this as a leader within your organization comes with some bad news . . . *Leadership is required* for all of this to work! Here are the primary things you need to focus on to make "the Innovators" successful and bring about the continuous improvement you hope to attain:

1.  Recognize when "Passion" or "Grit" exists and what the employee is passionate about and why . . . this requires observation and listening at all levels.

2.  When you find those employees who possess that passion and ability to create an improved business environment, *do something!* That means put them in a position where their success becomes the organization's success while helping them to feel their passion is being unleashed.

3. Recognize when "Grit" exists as a "trait" versus when it exists "situationally."

   a. Continue educating those who have "Grit" as a trait to become more knowledgeable about the company and apply their "Grit" more broadly.

   b. Continue challenging those who have "Grit" as a trait to ensure they can find a deeper passion for helping the company—not just a smaller segment of it.

   c. Make sure you fuel their fire, so they feel their worth to the company and want to continue applying their passion for *your* organization.

4. Hire properly to fuel future improvements within your organization. That means finding those knowledgeable enough about their areas of expertise and passionate enough about making it the best, and who left their previous organization because their leader could not do a, b, and c, above, to keep them motivated.

Piece of cake, right? It is not an easy task to build, nurture, challenge, and motivate a team.

This definitely qualifies as something worth doing. Taking the next step to work toward perfection in the building of your team is paramount. This is not something you want to find a shortcut for, for your sake and the sake of all the people you lead. Creating the right environment is important. Maybe we will get into that further together . . . hint, hint.

☊

STEP 9

# Changing Course . . . Rebuilding for the Future

*In this Step:*
- Using what we've learned so far
- Creating a Business Plan
- Assigning specific tasks
- Celebrating . . . successes and, yes, failures

**APPLYING WHAT IS LEARNED**

Before moving forward with the rebuilding process, I'd like to take a moment to recap one more time what we have discussed. The reason for doing this now (again) is that, before we start to blaze a new trail through the rebuilding process, we should take a quick glance over our shoulder. If this were a sprint to the finish line, I wouldn't recommend that. Remember, I've said that this is a marathon. In our attempt to rebuild your organization, team, or family into one you can accomplish great things with and through, I hope this recap provides a ready reference with which to navigate the process. The order of my summary matches the order of reference throughout the book . . . just in case it becomes helpful to go back and reread to remind yourself of certain points. Here is the recap of what we have discussed so far:

- ➤ We studied the health of your organization (both financially and culturally)
  - What motivates your organization toward its goals?
  - How does your organization spend its energy?
  - What is the state of your organization's goals?
  - What condition are your most important assets in?

- ➤ We discussed how an organization's culture can impact it . . . more specifically, *your* organization!
  - What is culture?
  - How does the culture impact your employees' motivation?
  - How do you align your culture with current conditions the organization faces?
  - What does culture's "Deep Roots" do for/to your organization?

- ➤ We discussed the ability to recognize when change to your culture is impacting your organization (positively/negatively)
  - When is your culture changing or collapsing, and what is the reason?
  - What is *not* the best way to promote culture and caring?
  - How do you recognize when your organization is changing (not in a good way)?

➤ We discussed having the ability to recognize when your organization has issues

- How did your organization's chemistry become compromised?
- Who/what is compromising your organization's balanced chemistry?
- What is the impact of avoiding conflict and not addressing the change?

➤ We discussed insights into your organization's chemistry

- How do you recognize and embrace differences in team members?
- How do you detect developing imbalances in the chemistry of your organization?
- What do you do to create the right chemical reaction within your organization?

➤ We discussed finding the right improvement opportunities in your organization

- What condition is your organization currently in?
- What are the opportunities for making the right improvements?
- Are you ready to drive change?

➤ We discussed how to start taking action to move in the right direction

- What will drive positive change and why?
- How you motivate the organization?
- How you position people in the right roles in the organization?
- How do you facilitate *my* organization's success?

> ➤ We discussed the role of "Grit" in a current or future member of the organization

- • What is "Grit"?
- • How does "Grit" compare to "Knowledge"?
- • How do I leverage "Grit" in the realignment of the organization?

My providing another recap is not insinuating that your memory or attention span is as lacking as mine, but maybe the summary above will serve a purpose as we venture into actually trying to make positive changes to the organization. It is also the foundation of the first portion of this Step of applying what has been learned.

The first thing I would recommend using in creating a new course for your organization is what we discussed in previous Steps . . . create a list of opportunities. If the assessments you have made during previous sections of this narrative were honest, deep, and broad, you likely have identified a number of improvement opportunities. As with any large undertaking, a massive list of action items can be very intimidating. Looking at all that needs to be done can actually become paralyzing and trigger procrastination. Don't let that happen. If the premise behind those statements sounds familiar, good! I touched on them in Step 6, but it is worth repeating. I already hinted at my next comment with the graphic in Step 6. I would recommend the addition of one more task at the beginning of your already-long list of things you identified to accomplish in order to achieve your goals (Great—make it even *more* intimidating). That new task I'm recommending would be to prioritize the list you have made before going forward! This would actually help to dissect the daunting task list and allow you to "eat the elephant one bite at a time" . . . to use an old saying. The process of prioritizing may also help you gain a better understanding of which items will create the greatest impact and further motivate the participants assigned to make it happen.

In creating a prioritized list of action items, there are a number of considerations to keep in mind. Making the actions match the organization's business objectives is one way to make sure the output of prioritizing makes sense to all assigned to execute it. Here are a few summarized points of consideration that might help make the prioritizing task a little more tolerable:

> Does the improvement give you a recognizable positive impact for the team, which brings benefit as well as an opportunity to celebrate a success as a team?

> If a prioritized item is a quick win with immediate benefit, does it align with my long-term goals and organizational objectives? If the answer is "Yes," it means it is a building block for the structure you are trying to create. If the answer is "No", this might imply it is just a "Band-Aid." If the action meets the immediate recognizable impact but must be reversed or eliminated with long-term actions, a different level of scrutiny must be applied. If the "Band-Aid' is necessary to solve a significant problem until a more complete solution is applied, proceeding with the temporary output may make sense. Sometimes a "Band-Aid" serves a purpose before fixing a problem altogether.

> Does the prioritized longer-term opportunity match where my business is *and* where I desire my business to be beyond the anticipated completion timeline? An example of this can be seen in the information technology (IT) world. If an organization lacks trained programmers in a development language, they shouldn't make a conscious decision to provide them with training on a language their insight tells them will be replaced in a year . . . at least I would hope not.

> ➤ How can you build a prioritized action plan that becomes self-sustaining? In a condition of limited cash flow, selecting actions that can generate financial benefit that can subsequently be used to fund future improvement opportunities is a good way not to be stalled by lack of funding. I have always referred to this as a "Pay as you go" model.

Regardless of the condition your company is in, these few criteria can be used to at least help start the conversation. Conditions within each company may be slightly to dramatically different. The ultimate driver for creating your priority opportunity list is to do what is best for your condition and organization.

In addition to the conditions you build your opportunity list with, there are a couple of things to keep in mind. The first is quite obvious. As I've stated before, the priority list of innovation opportunities should align with the organization's business plan. Making sure progress aligns with the direction of the organization should be one of the most important factors for moving forward. This is included in the considerations above in several places.

The second thing to consider is not focusing only on the short term. When constructing the organization's priority-action list, it should be done in conjunction with the organization's business plan. If the business plan doesn't exist or isn't clear, the priority list is a good starting point to create it or clarify it. (Spoiler Alert!) We are going to discuss that in the next section. I would liken the process of creating a prioritized improvement plan to transform your business without considering the business plan to building a boat without consideration of its ultimate use. Building an ocean-sailing craft with no self-propelling capability when the intended use is to navigate a river going upstream would not be a very productive use of resources. I know this is a ridiculous example, but I hope you understand the purpose for the analogy.

The use of a benefit-and-effort quadrant (see example) can be helpful to support ranking all of your improvement tasks and aid in your decision.

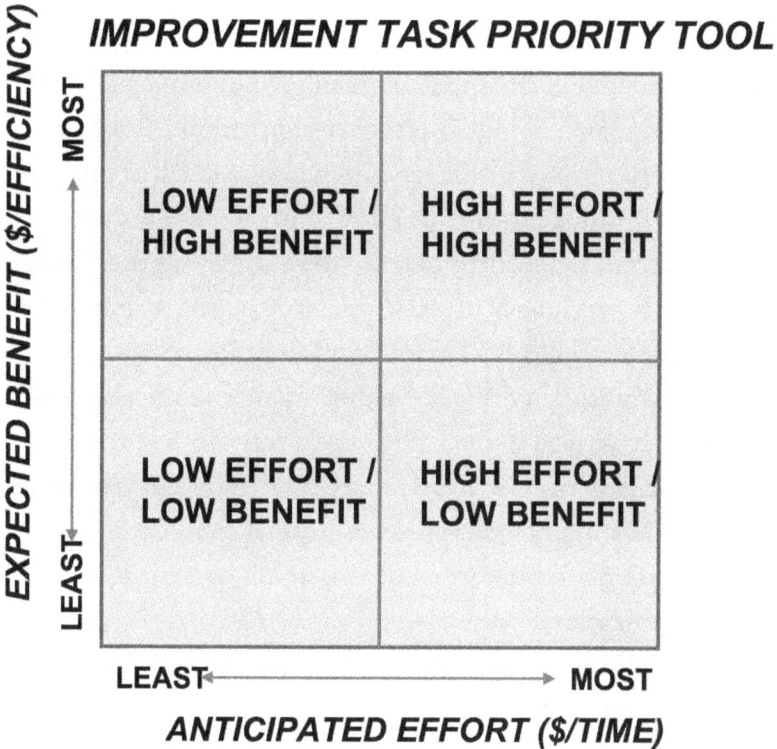

## IMPROVEMENT TASK PRIORITY TOOL

| | LOW EFFORT /<br>HIGH BENEFIT | HIGH EFFORT /<br>HIGH BENEFIT |
|---|---|---|
| | LOW EFFORT /<br>LOW BENEFIT | HIGH EFFORT /<br>LOW BENEFIT |

**EXPECTED BENEFIT ($/EFFICIENCY)** — MOST ↑ ... LEAST ↓

**ANTICIPATED EFFORT ($/TIME)** — LEAST ← → MOST

Placing each of the identified tasks in a quadrant based on how much time and/or money (estimated) and how much benefit you anticipate receiving, you will quickly see which tasks are best to focus on first. My word of caution for this process is to avoid falling into the trap of selecting *only* items in the Low Effort/High Benefit quadrant. Tasks that fall in the High Effort/Low Benefit quadrant may be required to be completed first in order to set a foundation for achieving your ultimate goals. If this is not the case, the Low Effort/High Benefit tasks may be your best priority to accomplish some quick wins to finance subsequent steps.

## CREATE THE BUSINESS PLAN

If you didn't gather from my "Spoiler Alert" comment in the last section that there would be an upcoming discussion on creating a business plan, then I didn't spoil the surprise. The purpose of this section is to define the method for creating your organization's business plan. For some of you in larger organizations, this may seem obvious. For some of you from medium-sized to small organizations, this may be totally foreign. For all of you, whether accustomed to creating an annual, multi-year, or 10-year (or another interval) business plan—or none at all—it doesn't mean you're doing it right. I won't profess to hold the secret ingredient for creating the most effective business plan. I won't claim this to be the only method for creating it, either. In the interest of continuous learning, I will offer my analogy of how you can create a solid business plan to support the setting of and approach toward challenging goals for your organization. I think you will also find it beneficial, regardless of your organization's size.

OK, this might sound a bit obvious, but the first thing you must do is give definition to the established objectives you feel are necessary to achieve reaching your "end in mind." Along with the desired outcomes you have established, you would create a good start to the business-planning process. The reason I've divided established objectives and desired outcomes is that I believe they are not always one and the same. My definition of a desired outcome is a state or condition targeted by the actions being undertaken in a business plan. In a word, you could view this as the "result" of what has been defined in the organization's business plan. My definition of established objectives would be the intermediate steps you take to finally reach the desired outcome. When you finally reach the "end in mind," the established objectives and desired outcomes may merge into one final measurable.

It is important, when you create a business plan, not to become confused by these two deliverables. I'll try to illustrate some examples to help you understand.

**EXAMPLE 1:**

This year, our business plan is to increase ROI to 10% ... Established Objective or Desired Outcome? If you think Desired Outcome, you paid attention to my definition. Achieving a 10% ROI would be what is being targeted through the actions defined in the organization's business plan. There would be a list of Established Objectives along the way to achieve that Outcome.

**EXAMPLE 2:**

This year, our business plan is to centralize buying to achieve a lower cost on our goods to improve our ROI .... Established Objective or Desired Outcome? If you think Established Objective, again you paid attention to my definition of the two. In this case the Desired Outcome would be the improvement of ROI. Side note: I would say the Outcome isn't well defined because there isn't a numeric target. It creates an optimal condition if you want not to be held too accountable. A .00001% improvement could mean the Outcome was met. I hope you agree with my assessment of the Outcome being too vague. That would tell me that you are in this to truly make a difference.

Now, to Confuse You:

Of the two examples I've provided, which Desired Outcome would you say could and should be measured as part of the organization's business plan? If you think both, you are right in line with my thinking. The Established Objectives should always be monitored and measured to ensure schedules and targets are being achieved. Otherwise, the Desired Outcome is not likely to be attained. Conversely, the Desired Outcomes should be measured to see if the Established Objectives are actually providing the benefits you thought they would. Keep in mind that the Desired Outcomes can be influenced by other outside factors despite your best efforts, so the measurements taken can be a bit ambiguous. Determining how to normalize (remove the outside influences to the best of your ability) the outputs—to take away those factors and see if the actions taken are consistent with what you thought you could achieve—is necessary. This will help to correctly monitor the results.

The last point I want to make about creating your organization's business plan is related to *How much do you put into it*? In my years in business, I have witnessed three basic schools of thought.

1. **Keep it simple, stupid**: Less is better when you create an organization's business plan. If there isn't that much committed to, there is less expectation to be met. If there are not many items in the business plan, there is less to report and explain. For this approach, a generic Outcome is great. Move the needle forward by a penny, and you've met the Objective.

   For the organization looking to "fly below the radar" and avoid being given more to do, this is a good approach. For the organization inside a company who is driven only by the results on a report and dishes out punishment to those who aren't filling in the results with "Happy Faces," "Green Dots," or "Check Marks," this is probably a good way to set up a business plan. It is all about self-preservation!

   Who wins in this scenario? The parties who scaled back their business plan to become an accomplished performer (but did they, really?).

   Who loses in this scenario? Everybody! Teams will underperform to their true capabilities. Apathy and stagnation abound. Everyone will look at the results from reporting and see that, despite all the organization performing well in their business plan Established Objectives, the Desired Outcomes may still not be met. Taking this approach will also not motivate the type of team you are trying to build.

2. **Match the Plan**: In a very calculated way, Established Objectives are carefully mapped out to meet the Desired Outcomes. On paper, it sounds like a match made in heaven. In a stable environment, where few outside influences impact the attainment of your Objectives and Outcomes, this is an acceptable way to establish an organization's business plan.

   For anyone who has been working through business plans for any length of time, would you like to inform everyone else how often Objectives are met without any interruptions? Oh, yeah—I guess *I* need to do that. The loss of a key contributor, an unplanned event occurring that requires the undivided attention of everyone, or something as simple as a series of small delays that add up to missing both Objectives and Outcomes can turn a year-end summary from "Look at what we did!" to "What have we done?" The impact from COVID-19 on virtually every business is a good example of the most extreme influence on business-plan activities and results.

   In the environment defined in the first approach, where "Smiley Face Ratings" and being chastised for missing targets abound, this would be the second-most-desirable approach to an organization. For an organization wanting to be recognized as a contributor, this might be their approach. Hint: This might motivate the type of team we are trying to build, but probably only for a short time.

3. **Above and Beyond**: This can best be defined as "over-filling the plate," based on normal expectations. Creating Objectives that deliver results greater than the "required" expectations

is a big part of setting a business plan in this way. There are many (dare I say, *most*) people who would describe this as insanity. In the right organizations, it can be a way to excel. For a leader who wishes to leave a legacy for all who follow, this is a way to achieve that.

This approach to creating a business plan can be undertaken only by those who want to "Soar." It is for those who step up to the plate and swing for the fences every time. Their belief is that there is no such thing as bad publicity. This is an organization where "Grit" abounds. The detriment of taking on potentially more than you can handle is that someone with the wrong mindset who views a failure during the journey as the end of the world could become discouraged. The benefit of taking on potentially more than you can handle is that everyone understands there is no place for idle time and loss of focus as long as they know the challenge. It also means that a few failures or delays within the Objectives do not necessarily equate to missing Outcomes.

There is a unique requirement necessary in the environment in which this organization dwells. The culture must be to celebrate both successes *and* temporary failures, where the effort was evident, but the Objectives were not achieved. Otherwise, the approach to accomplish more than your share will be met with nothing but unwise criticism and will create apathy among the team. It would be very easy for this motivated team to digress and take the approach of setting an easily attainable business plan, knowing all along they are living below their capability. This approach will challenge and motivate the type of team you are looking for.

The best way to describe what is necessary to get everyone performing (or over-performing) as described in the third example above would be to provide a supportive and nurturing culture. Everyone must understand their roles and the expectations of them, while also knowing the only time *trying* will be frowned upon is when it is "not trying." Be very cautious about establishing this type of environment. Side effects may be: continuous learning, excessive job satisfaction, sense of belonging to something special and willingness to go the extra mile for the organization/company/co-workers. Sound like someplace you might be interested in ~~working~~ belonging? The strikethrough was purposely left so you can understand the significance of finding this type of environment.

## ASSIGN DUTIES ... SPECIFIC, STRETCHED, SIGNIFICANT

Regardless of the approach taken to develop your business plan, the best way to ensure everyone knows their role in reaching the Established Objectives and attaining the Desired Outcomes is to create assignments for each of them. This helps in two separate, yet connected, ways. All parties gain understanding of the direction the organization is taking, and they also gain insight into how their actions affect and contribute to reaching the desired result. Talk about feeling important as an individual and being part of the team—this would certainly facilitate that.

In keeping with the approach to develop a business plan that could be deemed beyond the capabilities of an organization, the assignment of duties must take a similar approach. The assignment of the business-plan items can take on a couple of different methods.

One method of assigning business-plan ownership is summed up very well in the old adage stated several ways and attributed to several people. The essence of the quote is: "If you want something done, ask a busy person." Personally, I've led numerous people and organizations who fit this mold. Regardless of how much they had going on, if they felt an important task was being entrusted to them, they would never say "No." The "Yes" might be followed by an expletive, but the reality behind their answer to accept the responsibility is that they are flattered by this kind of trust in their abilities.

It is important that a leader watch carefully to ensure that outside influences don't become overwhelming. It is also important to maintain an open environment, where that individual or group of individuals feel they can come directly to the leader to have an honest conversation when they find accomplishing the task has become impossible. Can you guess what approach those types of organizations take to build their business plans? I bet you can! (Hint: It's #3)

Another method is to assign business-plan actions to those who are most qualified. This is a solid approach, but only to a certain extent. The most qualified are not always the most motivated. If there are members in your organization who are both qualified and motivated, give them all the opportunities they can manage. Mutual benefits can be gained when this condition exists. The individual can benefit from seeing, feeling, and knowing the impact of their actions. The downside of assigning activities only to those who are knowledgeable and capable is that the rest of the organization cannot obtain the growth you hope to facilitate through experience. Partnering someone who possesses the motivation but not the knowledge with a person who has both can support achievement of that growth as well as help the parties taking on the workload maintain some work-life balance.

Conversely, as seen through my personal observations of working with busy people who don't mind being busier, I've also led individuals and organizations who were satisfied with their capabilities alone. A feeling of "There is nothing for me to prove" can exist and persist. These teams are much more likely to underachieve to their personal capabilities. I'm guessing you have a good understanding of this organization's approach to establishing their business plan. If you said they will commit to just enough to ensure they can achieve everything they committed to, you're getting the hang of it!

If you find you are experiencing a very similar situation of team members being satisfied with their capability in your own organizations, it can become tough to stack your business plan with bigger contributions. There is one team who is ready to take on the world, whether they have the skills or not, and another who has the skills but doesn't want to over-apply themselves. Hmmm, how do you fix that? Back to the chemistry lesson . . . start mixing the resources until you find the right chemical reaction to motivate both teams and raise everyone's knowledge. Sounds simple, doesn't it? Not really, but if you are an overachieving personality, you will figure it out and not give up until you do. Another "Rock Tumbler" opportunity!

> *"If everyone is moving forward together, then success takes care of itself."* —Henry Ford

Success in assigning business-plan activities can be achieved through everyone working in lockstep toward the known and common goals. Success in motivating your team will come from ensuring "busy hands" within the organization, which can achieve successes beyond what they may have felt they could achieve. Success in moving members of your organization in the right direction within the "Success Box" (detailed previously) will come from their excitement brought about by successes and belief—"I Can" and "I'll Try."

## CELEBRATE SUCCESSES . . . *AND* FAILURES

With the differing approaches mentioned before about how business plans can be developed, there was a key factor I hope you picked up on. The environment the leadership of an organization creates can have a profound impact on the motivation of members of the organization and the approach they take in challenging themselves or their teams. This may sound a bit obvious, but it doesn't seem to be considered in many organizations. As I mentioned, if the environment is that of only managing to metrics, someone missing a deadline or expected result might be chastised and/or punished (less-than-optimal performance rating, less-than-optimal raise, or even demotion). Instead of looking at the accomplishments they did achieve and understanding that the team put more on their plates than others, it is just about the numbers! That would be like a parent rewarding an equally talented child for getting an "A" in remedial math and punishing the other, equally talented child for getting a "B" in an advanced-math program. "Why can't you be more like your sibling and get all A's?" I know that really sounds silly, but if you think it doesn't happen in business (or families), you might be surprised.

So, what does this all have to do with you? As a leader or a parent, it is important to establish an environment where everyone can be comfortable in reaching for the stars. As with those who possess "Grit," your organization (business, team, family) will begin to believe that failure doesn't define them ... and it doesn't hurt them! Provided the effort has been made and the commitment to not give up until they achieve success is there, the failure will be recognized as only Phase 1 ... there is much more to come. Being able to create that type of environment in your organization will be followed by the opportunity for great successes.

Successes, whether from a first attempt or follow-up attempts, must be celebrated. Whether it is a party, a bonus, or just a simple "Thank you," don't let that opportunity slip by. That is the obvious part of this chapter. The less-obvious part of this chapter is the celebration of the unsuccessful attempts taken. Celebration? ... Of failures? ... Yes! Think about it. A person or group of people who just legitimately poured themselves into trying to do something great are the most vulnerable to start second-guessing themselves in the event their targeted results aren't achieved. Having someone recognize their effort, despite the outcome, and letting them know there is still confidence in their reaching the Outcome through persistence can re-light the passion within them. Celebrate the effort without losing sight of the missed Desired Outcome.

> *"In great attempts, it is glorious even to fail."* —*Cassius Longinus*

A good leader will teach through their actions (as described above) that failure is a significant part of life! Actions truly do speak louder than words. A word of caution ... an interesting dynamic may occur as you do this. If a leader acting in this way is out of character, based on past history, there is going to be some skepticism on the part of the organization's members. A feeling that "I'm being set up for something" or "What are they up to?" might pop into their minds. You might want to warn them why you are suddenly happy they tried even if they failed!

A good leader should also be willing to teach through their failures. When words can speak equally as loud as actions is when someone can openly and honestly share their own experiences (most notably, their failures). As I mentioned before, I hope I can share some of my painful failures with my grandchildren, so they gain that knowledge without experiencing the same pain I endured. I'm guessing all those lessons won't be taken at face value, but hopefully some are. The same holds true for sharing business failures that you've experienced. Looking back at the many I've experienced personally, I know that they made me stronger and wiser. And yes ... sometimes they can be embarrassing. Sharing them with my teams let them know I'm human.

Keeping that last statement in mind, it is good to keep as part of your "lesson" to others that, in life, it is natural to have both successes and failures. The failures are OK! Please don't misread that statement or get the impression that it is made in the context of what is going on among youth sports. It *doesn't* mean that everyone gets a trophy. It *doesn't* mean that the expectations have been lowered to the level of the current outcome. It *does* mean that failure should motivate you to do better the next time. It *does* mean that you can be disappointed with the Outcome but not discouraged to a point of not being willing to work both harder and smarter the next time. It *does* mean that you have a new hurdle to overcome, and there is a belief it can be overcome.

To keep all the discussion of failure in context, there is an expectation of the failure itself. That expectation is that the failure should be your teacher. The lesson is that of learning through the mistakes made or identifying when the difficulty was underestimated. I once heard a Youth Travel Baseball Coach make an expectation known to his players. He told them: "Don't compound a mistake with a mistake." His definition was to explain to his players not to try to do something they weren't capable of to make up for a mistake. The outcome was likely going to be a failure on top of the previous failure. The lesson we can all take away from that is to learn from the first mistake so as not to repeat it. Don't let that educational opportunity go to waste!

If you can accomplish learning from both failures *and* successes, your approach is going to become something like this:

Don't Repeat Failures, Build on Successes . . . Don't Repeat Failures, Build on Successes . . . Rinse and Repeat! If you can accomplish this formula, as well as promote it within your teams, you are going to like the results! If you, yourself, can understand that every moment, every action, every outcome is an educational opportunity and teach that to your teams, you will create growth in every member. This all may be obvious to some, but not to everyone! *It can be very powerful!*

☊

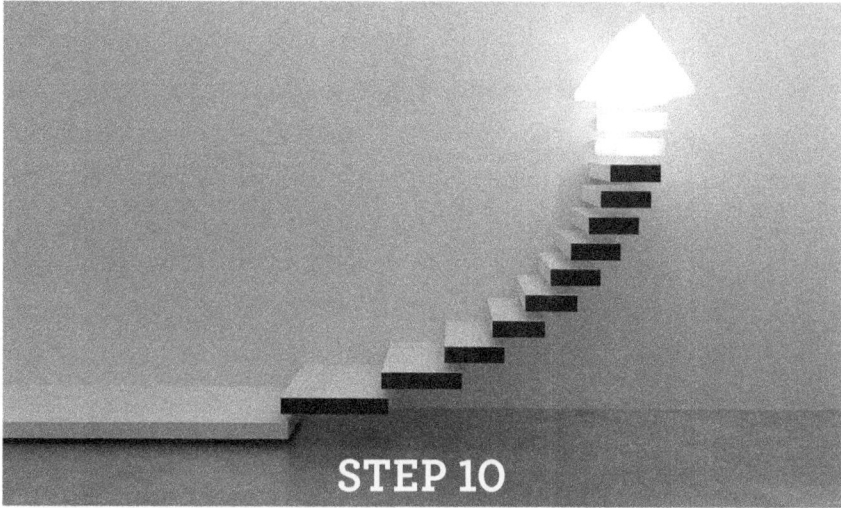

**STEP 10**

# Assess the Success

*In this Step:*
- Learn how things went
- Make the process your own
- Don't quit!

## ASSESSING "HOW THINGS WENT"

Now that you have finished the first 9 Steps and gone through the journey of looking into how your business or maybe even yourself is doing and made the changes that make it and/or you better—or possibly, even *great*—you are finished! Congratulations!....

Okay, okay, you knew better than that. You probably could surmise there is more based on what I've stated throughout the content of this book . . . not to mention the title and lead-in for this Step. The reality is that you aren't finished. If you have been successful during most of the exercises mentioned, you are really on your way and just getting started. I would love to be able to help you along through the next steps of this marathon. To do that, you will just have to read my next book . . .

... *not!* Actually, if you understood or picked up on the formulas throughout the content of this book, you are already armed with the knowledge and methods to keep running the marathon. To return to a sports analogy of a competing runner, the best coaches will likely tell you to never look back over your shoulder. That is a true statement when you are competing against others. Keep plowing ahead, and don't look back. Relax only when you have crossed the finish line. That advice isn't as sound when you are running a "business- or personal-growth marathon." It is good to look back, especially when you have come this far.

As you enter the next phase of discovery and innovation, it may become very easy to get weary or distracted or (and here is the ultimate buzzkill) *satisfied!* I have mentioned how an employee who becomes "satisfied" is one who ceases to grow. That is true for yourself as well. A true, finely tuned competitor learns that when they reach that state, they have come to the point when they must draw on pure adrenaline and let the muscle memory kick in. For a runner leading a race, looking back over their shoulder shouldn't be where their adrenaline is derived. They know their competitors are back there. It is derived from what is *ahead* of them—the finish line. The opportunity to be recognized as the best (at least on that given day and race). The personal satisfaction of achieving what they had trained for and set out to do.

It is a little bit different for someone leading a company.

I'm going to start by saying that my next statements have some assumptions involved. They assume you and your team have successfully put into practice some or all of the thoughts I've shared with you and have seen some successes from it. They assume that you are still reading and truly want to see if there is more! More opportunities! More options! More successes! More work?

This next statement will make every track coach across the globe cringe. Take time to look over your shoulder, and witness what you've accomplished. I don't hesitate to give this advice, because, unlike running a business, someone running a race won't typically have unknown obstacles in front of them that require them to change course. A marathoner doesn't find out someone decided to add a 5% grade to the last 5 miles of their course (likened to a new government requirement put on your business) or being told they have to run the final mile pulling a wagon (likened to having an unexpected setback requiring your immediate attention). Their need for adrenaline and focusing on finishing the race are solely about themselves.

For those of us in business, seeing the success and remembering how it made you and others in your organization feel will give you that adrenaline boost to want to do more. It can provide that burst of energy needed to face unknown challenges and adapt. When things are going well because of the accomplishments of the past and a lack of unplanned-for obstacles, it becomes easy to be *satisfied.* If you look back and remember how it made you feel to accomplish things, regardless of how big or small, you may resist the temptation of becoming *satisfied* with where the organization is today. Adapting when a sudden change takes place is one thing. Anticipating changes and using the successes you encounter to prepare for them (of course, in moderation) facilitates moving from firefighting to fire prevention. That is a great day! *Celebrate!*

So, where does that leave us? The best advice I can give you at this point is to repeat the Process! You will likely find that, as you go back through the Assessment, Cultural Review, Resource Review, Team Chemistry Review, Opportunity Assessment, Team Conditions, and Path Forward Process, your findings will look much different from the last time. How much different and how much less frightening they are will depend on how successful you were the prior time(s). They will also vary based on the reason behind retracing the steps. If the purpose for repeating is that you *want* to, the result will likely be different than if it is because something has changed, and you *have* to. So will the required effort and timeline . . . depending on the demands and expectations you place on yourself.

As you progress through multiple iterations of the process, the amount of time and effort required may vary greatly. Doing a deep dive because the conditions you are facing require it may take you back to the same amount of effort spent the first time. The process should still be easier because of the experience you have gained and the confidence inspired by past successes. Adapting to a minor change may appear to be effortless because of the conditions and your experience. You may not even be aware the process was repeated.

Regardless of the reason for taking the journey again, remember it is all about continuously moving the needle in a positive direction. Just like with a gas tank, if you start from "Empty," it takes a lot to get to "Full." Each time positive steps are taken the gas gauge moves closer to a *full* state. If the first attempt at this endeavor allows your organization to reach a "¾ *full*" status, the next time may feel more like topping off the tank.

## MAKE IT YOUR OWN

As the section title indicates, every circumstance, whether a small business, large corporation, or business team, will present itself differently. Taking into account the external factors, which are infinitesimally different, you could expect that no two journeys through this process will be exactly alike. The base approach and beginning steps may be. That is what you should make your own.

To provide an example: a larger corporation may build a task force of leaders from different disciplines within the organization to lead the company through this type of journey. The task force approach probably isn't going to work for a small business team . . . just saying! Conversely, the approach a small business team might take, such as a weekly quiet-time meeting to discuss with equal voices, probably isn't going to make any progress in a large company or even a medium-sized business.

The entire point is that there isn't a magic formula I can provide to make every process look alike, and neither can you. If I could, a) I would be quite wealthy (I'm not, in monetary terms), and b) I would likely never retire and just continue to assist businesses in reaching their own Nirvana (that isn't going to happen). Each organization will probably find that circumstantial influences will dictate a slightly different approach, and they should adapt to them. Imagine if our approach toward going to work each day had to follow the same plan and pattern. Get up at a certain time, get ready the same way, get in your vehicle and leave at the same time, drive the exact same route to arrive at work by a certain time, and clock in (if that is required). That probably sounds pretty much right for most of us.

Where I'm going with this is what would you do if a road along your normal route is closed for construction? For 30 days! You wouldn't declare the process broken and failed, turn around, go back to your home, and stay there for 30 days until the road is back open! I know, another extreme example (and silly), but it makes the point for adapting the approach to the circumstances and continuing on. Someone or something throws up a roadblock that makes your approach ineffective; you rethink a portion of your steps and continue on. Now you have a slightly different playbook for future journeys. You made the approach your own!

As I stated in my "Acknowledgements", sharing my thoughts through this writing has taken me a lot longer than I had planned. That makes me feel a bit like an underachiever. However, my procrastination has brought about a number of additional life "observations" that both drove me to finish and provided examples to share.

No one event provides more examples than the Coronavirus pandemic, which continues at the time of my completion of this writing, but it's getting better. Watching the events unfold provides evidence of what I've stated in previous Steps. From applying different forms of "Drivers" based on what the conditions require for adapting the strategy as the conditions change or as improved data becomes available, many of the principles can be witnessed. The key difference is that the success or failure of this undertaking has a much higher impact . . . our nation's lives and livelihoods.

Lacking any type of blueprint to follow brings about the opportunity for innovation and reinvention to be used to navigate through uncertainties. Both are on display in many formats. Whether it is reinventing the process for gaining approval of new tools or approaches to fight the virus faster than ever thought possible, or the innovation shown to develop them, it should inspire you. If this type of possibility exists for government with the partnership of the private sector, it is certainly possible for your organization. If a government at a federal level has been able to achieve speeds never thought possible, think what you can do! Also on display is a lack of the same government to adapt to new facts and conditions and change the approach when it warrants. The playbook is the playbook, whether it is working or not!

Unfortunately, additionally on display is the presence of pollutants. In Step 4, I mentioned several "personalities" that become pollutants to a healthy organization. For the sake of brevity, I'll roll many of those personalities up into a new one . . . The Armchair Quarterback. When I think of an armchair quarterback, I see an overweight person sitting back in their easy chair with the remote in one hand and a beer in the other—someone who has neither the ability to be in the position they are second-guessing nor the "Grit." It is easy for an armchair quarterback to second-guess someone who has made a decision while in the throes of a stressful situation when the armchair quarterback has the aid of "replay" available to them. These armchair quarterbacks come in the form of political rivals, media, and pundits (anyone else recognize the irony of having the word "stupid" imbedded in the letters which make up "pundits"?). In any event, reforming or removing those pollutants is the only way to make the necessary improvements. Hmmm ... maybe my next book could be about the culture of Washington or politics in general. Naw ... probably already exists. Maybe a book on Unintended Consequences?!

The takeaway from this is that there are many lessons to be learned from every attempt to evaluate your organization to make improvements or tackle a situation like the Coronavirus. Learning from each process undertaken will make the next round that much easier ... relatively speaking. Using the new knowledge acquired from the previous exercise and tailoring the approach to the conditions being tackled will provide the best formula for success. If you think that once a journey is ended, it is *the end* of the *journey*, that would be the worst possible approach (and couldn't be farther from the truth). Ending one journey should be looked at as closing one door and discovering another standing ajar.

## Don't Ever Stop

By my previous comment that the journey isn't over when you end a journey, you can probably guess what I mean by this section's title. It is best to adopt a "tinkerer's" approach. In an environment where a product is competing with other companies' products, is it wise to stop product development? Of course not. Once a product launch is achieved (end of a journey of sorts), it is not time to sit back and take the approach of "We are finished" (end of the final journey). The competition is not going to surrender! The customer is not going to take the attitude that "It just doesn't get any better than this!" You'd better start working even harder to make sure you continue to develop the product to stay ahead of both the competition and customer expectations.

The same holds true for managing the company environment and culture. Remember, good enough is never good enough! If you are involved in the type of environment that never changes, congratulations! *Really, congratulations!* Guess you can't catch the sarcasm based on how I write it. Maybe it will help to state the only environment I know of that is not susceptible to change is . . . well, none! Change is a fact of every life and every business. No matter how much we try to ignore or avoid it, it isn't possible. Remember, if you want to know the future, make it. That would be the motto of every "disruptor." No true disruptor (regardless of the circumstance) wants to wait for someone else to decide the future.

The best advice, coming from a change agent (disruptor of sorts), is to embrace the fact that the one constant in life is change. Learning to adapt to any circumstance and recognize it for what it is . . . another opportunity to shine . . . will serve you well. Being able to share that trait with others around you will serve you even more. Creating a culture of change is something very unique in virtually all businesses. Those who have adapted and adopted it are likely set to overachieve. Taking that approach of continually assessing how your business is doing is no exception. Whether it is an established cadence to evaluate how your culture is doing, or whether it's triggered by some key performance metric (turnover rate, customer complaints, productivity numbers), this activity should be viewed in the same light as product development. After all, whether you believe it or not, you are in competition for your employees' loyalty. In an age where company loyalty is not as important as in the past, it is important to set yourself apart. A sincere attempt to listen and improve is a good step toward that.

As you continue to assess, reassess, and re-reassess the health of your organization, don't forget to continuously adapt the structure of the approach to the conditions faced. Sometimes that approach will be to maintain the current conditions. That means the outside influences are not overwhelming and that the internal conditions are welcomed by everyone. That circumstance may be less likely, but it can happen. Sometimes the approach will be to innovate. This is the more likely circumstance. Outside influences exist, and to keep the internal conditions in a desired state, action will be needed to adapt. Sometimes the approach requires reinvention. When the outside influences become extreme, a more invasive approach is the best or only option. Don't be afraid to use it! If that all sounded familiar, you've been listening.

One final word of advice: It will never be possible to make everyone happy. Don't try! I've learned over time that someone who tries to be all things to all people can be called a lot of things . . . conflicted, tired, *crazy*. Ultimately, the best descriptor would be *unsuccessful*. In business, the logical solution for addressing when a company and/or its culture doesn't match an employee's expectation is easy . . . part ways. That is when the rocks in the tumbler wear on each other; it becomes an adapted approach that may result in a compromise. The rounded rock which emerges from the tumbler is more likely to be able to "roll with the changes." Regardless, some type of action and some type of change is the best approach.

I sincerely hope that sharing my personal experiences through these writings provides a new or sometimes validating opinion for everyone who has absorbed it. I also hope you derive many benefits from reading it. My personal goal for creating the content was to share the experiences and observations I was fortunate enough to obtain from my many years of working in a number of environments. If you got a little enjoyment out of it as well, my wife may say your sense of humor is as warped as mine. Guess that isn't all that bad. After all, we can't all be "normal"! Some of us have to accomplish something!

Best wishes and good luck in your "Journey" regardless of how big or small and whether it takes place in the office or the home.

Don't let obstacles stop you! Stay true to your values! Remember that the people around you can make you better!

> *"Never lose sight of the fact that the most important yardstick of your success will be how you treat other people."* —*Barbara Bush*

◑

# About the Author

Dana McBrien spent the bulk of his career managing numerous segments within Honda's North America manufacturing supply chain. During his tenure at Honda, McBrien and his teams' efforts focused on managing the operations as well as continuously improving the domestic and international supply chain while building resiliency against the many disruptions. Many of those efforts toward continuous improvement were well documented in an Automotive Logistics Magazine interview (July–September 2015). In addition to his Honda responsibilities, he maintained an active affiliation with the Automotive Industry Action Group and frequently participated in speaking and panel discussions for the Automotive Logistics Magazine Global Conference.

After 34+ years with Honda, McBrien retired in 2018. Upon retirement, he began consulting with an emphasis on creating the best supply chain management processes and solutions. Utilizing the broad knowledge gained from the disciplines he experienced or managed during his professional career (accounting, banking, finance, manufacturing, material planning, supplier relations, solutions development and implementation, transportation, logistics, and supply chain) has aided in that process.

McBrien resides in Ohio with Lora, his wife of over 35 years. When not playing tennis, he enjoys spending time with his family, including two grown children, their spouses, and their growing families.

www.ingramcontent.com/pod-product-compliance
Lightning Source LLC
Chambersburg PA
CBHW031853200326
41597CB00012B/396